The Tyndale New Testament Commentaries

General Editor: PROFESSOR R. V. G. TASKER, M.A., D.D.

THE EPISTLES OF PAUL
TO THE COLOSSIANS
AND PHILEMON

THE EPISTLES OF PAUL TO THE

COLOSSIANS

AND

PHILEMON

AN INTRODUCTION AND COMMENTARY

by

HERBERT M. CARSON, B.A., B.D.

INTER-VARSITY PRESS

© INTER-VARSITY PRESS

Inter-Varsity Fellowship
39 Bedford Square, London WC1B 3EY

First Edition - February 1960
Reprinted - May 1963
Reprinted - January 1966
Reprinted - March 1968
Reprinted - May 1970
Reprinted - January 1974

HARDBACK EDITION 0 85111 609 4
PAPERBACK EDITION 0 85111 804 6

PRINTED IN GREAT BRITAIN BY
BILLING AND SONS LTD
GUILDFORD AND LONDON

GENERAL PREFACE

ALL who are interested in the teaching and study of the New Testament today cannot fail to be concerned with the lack of commentaries which avoid the extremes of being unduly technical or unhelpfully brief. It is the hope of the editor and publishers that this present series will do something towards the supply of this deficiency. Their aim is to place in the hands of students and serious readers of the New Testament, at a moderate cost, commentaries by a number of scholars who, while they are free to make their own individual contributions, are united in a common desire to promote a truly biblical theology.

The commentaries are primarily exegetical and only secondarily homiletic, though it is hoped that both student and preacher will find them informative and suggestive. Critical questions are fully considered in introductory sections, and also, at the author's discretion, in additional notes.

The commentaries are based on the Authorized (King James) Version, partly because this is the version which most Bible readers possess, and partly because it is easier for commentators, working on this foundation, to show why, on textual and linguistic grounds, the later versions are so often to be preferred. No one translation is regarded as infallible, and no single Greek manuscript or group of manuscripts is regarded as always right! Greek words are transliterated to help those unfamiliar with the language, and to save those who do know Greek the trouble of discovering what word is being discussed.

There are many signs today of a renewed interest in what the Bible has to say and of a more general desire to understand its meaning as fully and clearly as possible. It is the hope of all those concerned with this series that God will graciously use what they have written to further this end.

R. V. G. TASKER.

CONTENTS

CHIEF ABBREVIATIONS

AV	English Authorized Version (King James).
RV	English Revised Version, 1881.
RSV	American Revised Standard Version, 1946.
B	Codex Vaticanus.
LXX	Septuagint Version.
Abbott	*Commentary on Ephesians and Colossians* (The International Critical Commentary).
Alford	*The Greek Testament* by Henry Alford, 1857.
C. F. D. Moule	*Commentary on Colossians and Philemon* by C. F. D. Moule (The Cambridge Greek Testament) 1957.
H. C. G. Moule	*Colossian and Philemon Studies* by Handley C. G. Moule.
Lightfoot	*The Epistles of St. Paul: III—The First Roman Captivity* by J. B. Lightfoot, 1927.
Olshausen	*Biblical Commentary on Galatians, Ephesians, Colossians and Thessalonians* by Hermann Olshausen (Clark's Foreign Theological Library), 1851.
Wordsworth	*Commentary on St. Paul's Epistles* by Christopher Wordsworth, 1868.

AUTHOR'S PREFACE

THIS commentary originated in a series of sermons preached in the ordinary course of steady exposition in the pulpit of a parish church. It has been continued and completed in the same context. As a result there is an inevitable concern—even if at times subconsciously—with the preacher's task. If it makes some small contribution to the revival of expository preaching in the Church, the labour involved in its production will be more than repaid.

The Epistle to the Colossians is essentially Christ centred. Faced with the spread of false teaching, Paul turns believers' minds and hearts to the Person and work of Christ, with whose glory he himself is so taken up. For this reason it has a message for the Church in every age, and possibly especially for our own day. Amid all the cross currents of thinking and practice in the Church at large, there is need for a firm re-assertion of the Lordship of Christ who alone is Head of the Church, and whose Word must be the final authority.

But what is true for the Church as a whole is true also for the individual believer. So often the welter of theories has confused rather than helped in the quest for holiness. There is need surely for a fresh realization of what it means to be *in Christ*. Paul's constant use of this phrase, with his vivid awareness of the riches which are the believer's inheritance, should drive us back to examine afresh the glory of our standing as new men *in Him*.

In attempting to comment on this Epistle I have of course followed in the footsteps of many whose labours and devotion have enriched our understanding of the Word, and from whom I have learned much. I would also pay tribute to those whose fellowship has stimulated an attempt to get to grips with the text. To the members of the Westminster Fellowship and especially to Dr. Martyn Lloyd-Jones I owe a debt I shall never fully repay. For the stimulus to truly biblical thinking given by membership of that fellowship—*soli Deo gloria.*

HERBERT M. CARSON.

INTRODUCTION

I. THE CHURCH AT COLOSSAE

COLOSSAE was one of a group of three cities in the Lycus valley of which the other two were Laodicea and Hierapolis. As they were only a short distance apart, close contact between the different communities was inevitable and this is reflected in the Epistle. Thus Paul includes the believers in Laodicea as those for whom he prays (ii. 1) and both Laodicea and Hierapolis are named in connection with the labours of Epaphras (iv. 13). Then again the regular intercourse between the cities would facilitate the exchange of letters enjoined by the apostle (iv. 16). Laodicea was the most important of the three, being the chief city of the region. By contrast, Colossae at this period was a small town over-shadowed by its wealthy neighbours, and certainly not a place of any great significance.

It seems most unlikely that Paul had visited any of these cities. The record of his missionary journeys in Acts has no mention of them; and indeed he states that they had not seen his face (ii. 1). Wordsworth, it is true, in his comment on this verse claims that Paul here is really contrasting those in Colossae and Laodicea who have seen him with those elsewhere who have not seen him. But this is rather forced as there is no hint of a contrast in the verse, for the three groups are simply linked together by the conjunction 'and'. It seems more likely that the gospel had come to the region through the agency of Paul's converts. Thus Epaphras is the one who taught them the gospel (i. 7) and Philemon, in whose house the church meets, is himself a convert of Paul (Phm. 19). The prolonged stay in Ephesus during the third missionary journey had led to a far-reaching ministry so that Luke can say that 'all they which dwelt in Asia heard the word of the Lord Jesus, both Jews and Greeks' (Acts xix. 10). It is highly probable that it was in Ephesus that Epaphras had heard the gospel which he himself received and then took back to Colossae which was his home (iv. 12).

II. THE AUTHORSHIP OF COLOSSIANS

There are two main questions here. Did Paul himself write the Epistle; and, if so, where was he at the time of writing? As far as the Pauline authorship is concerned the arguments against it are not very convincing. Peculiarities of language are quite explicable in view of the special circumstances with which he is dealing, and the specific error which he is refuting. Nor can we argue that the heresy at Colossae savours of second-century Gnosticism. It is true that we have in germ the errors which were afterwards to be fully developed by the Gnostic sects; but at this stage such terms as *plērōma*, *teleios*, and *gnōsis* are not used in their later developed meaning. Their usage in this Epistle is quite consistent with a first-century writing.

A modern variant of the attack on the Pauline authorship is put forward by Charles Masson.[1] He adopts the view of Holtzman that the canonical Epistle to the Colossians is a development of a primitive Epistle of Paul. This original letter was brief because of his imprisonment, but was later expanded by the author of the Epistle to the Ephesians. So Masson is only prepared to concede that 'the epistle in this sense is Pauline'. He contends that in the present Epistle we have an elaboration of doctrine which is foreign to the authentic Epistles of Paul. But in reply we might point out that while in Paul's writings there is a development, the doctrines expounded in Colossians follow naturally from teaching in other Epistles. Thus in the very doctrine cited by Masson as an alien elaboration of Pauline teaching, namely the teaching on the Church which receives life and unity from the Head, we are surely moving in the same realm of thought as I Corinthians xii. 12 ff. or Romans xii. 5. Similarly the Christo-

---

[1] *L'Épître de Saint Paul aux Colossiens* (Commentaire du Nouveau Testament), Vol. x.

logy of the Epistle has close affinities with that of Philippians ii. 6 or I Corinthians viii. 6; and his teaching on the cross in ii. 14, 15 recalls Galatians iii. 13 or 2 Corinthians v. 19–21.

In favour of the Pauline authorship is the obvious similarity between this Epistle and that to Philemon which clearly comes from the hand of the apostle. This similarity is so marked that a common authorship must be presupposed. We might note the following characteristics. In both cases Timothy is his companion. His other companions also appear in both letters—Epaphras, Aristarchus, Mark, Demas and Luke. In both letters Archippus appears as the recipient of a message. In the letter to Colossae the section on the treatment of slaves with its fuller detail reflects the main theme of the letter to Philemon. In both cases the writer is in prison (Col. iv. 3, 18; Phm. 1, 9). In the letter to Colossae, Tychicus who bears the letter is accompanied by Onesimus, the subject of the short accompanying note. The conclusion is inescapable. Both letters came from the same author—the apostle Paul.

Where then was Paul when he wrote these letters? To this question various answers have been given—Caesarea, Ephesus and Rome. The only argument in favour of Caesarea is the fact of Paul's prolonged imprisonment which lasted for over two years (Acts xxiv. 27). But would Paul in mentioning his various companions ignore the presence of Philip the evangelist who had been his host at Caesarea not so long before (Acts xxi. 8)? Indeed Caesarea seems to be completely excluded by Paul's message to Philemon that he is hoping shortly to visit Colossae, for when he was in Caesarea his aim was rather to visit Rome (cf. Acts xxiii. 11).

A much stronger case can be made out in favour of Ephesus.[1] The argument is developed along these lines. Paul associates with him in the Epistle Timothy, the companion of his third missionary journey when Ephesus was his base. He refers to the possibility of visiting Asia again whereas, during his Roman imprisonment, his aim was to go on to Spain (Rom. xv. 28). He is obviously in close contact with Colossae, from

[1] G. S. Duncan, *St. Paul's Ephesian Ministry*, London, 1929.

which he has received news; but this is unlikely if he was as far away as Rome. Then again, Onesimus would be more likely to go to the nearby Ephesus than to the remote capital of the Empire. The situation at Colossae is that of a church of recent origin, which would favour Paul's still exercising his rather lengthy Ephesian ministry. If the Epistle to the Philippians belongs to the same period it is still possible to postulate Ephesus. The *praetorium* (Phil. i. 13) was the customary Latin word for the government house in the provinces, and the household of Caesar (Phil. iv. 22) referred to those engaged in the personal service of the Emperor whether at Rome or elsewhere.

But in spite of these admittedly strong arguments the claims of Rome seem even stronger. There is no clear evidence of an Ephesian imprisonment. Acts is silent on the subject, whereas, of course, it records the imprisonment at Rome (xxviii. 30). Duncan tries to establish such a period in Ephesus as an inference from various statements of the apostle. But in none of these references (Rom. xvi. 3, 7; 1 Cor. iv. 9, xv. 30–32; 2 Cor. i. 8–10) can we find a clear statement of a specific imprisonment, and certainly not one of any duration. Unless one had a theory to support, the evidence mustered from these verses would scarcely be regarded as sufficient to overthrow the silent witness of Acts. It is surely inconceivable that Luke could have been with Paul at the time of the penning of these Epistles and have left no record. Duncan attempts to deal with this silence in Acts by the rather doubtful expedient of analysing Luke's motives in writing. Thus, he says, Luke wrote to commend Christianity to the imperial authorities. But the proconsul in Ephesus, Junius Silanus, was put to death as a possible rival of Nero. Hence it would have been impolitic to include any reference to Silanus. But even were we to accept this view of Luke's motive we might as readily turn the argument the other way. If Paul were imprisoned under Silanus then surely the latter could have been represented as the foe of the gospel as well as of the Emperor, and so the Christian message have been commended! Furthermore Luke seems to have been absent during Paul's ministry in Ephesus, for the 'we' passages in Acts do not appear from Acts xvi. 17 to xx. 5, whereas he is one of Paul's companions at the time of the writing of the Epistle to the Colossians.

As far as the other arguments are concerned they are easily met. Onesimus was just as likely to flee to Rome, where indeed there was more chance of escape than at Ephesus, which was really a little too close to his old home. The ease of communication between Rome and the distant parts of the empire disposes of the difficulty as to how Paul so easily got news of Colossae. Nor can the church have been of such recent origin, for some time must have elapsed for error to creep in. Paul's references to Epaphras suggest that the latter's authority or character was being impugned. But this is hardly likely at a very early stage when he was the bearer of the good news of salvation. As far as Paul's declared intention to visit Spain is concerned, it is quite possible that the news which reached him of the growth of error in Asia Minor should have led him to a change of plans.

The most likely time then for the writing of the Epistle was during his first imprisonment at Rome. If we are to allow time for his companions to join him in Rome we may suppose that it was towards the end of his imprisonment. This is confirmed by his expressed hope of an early release. The date of the Epistle will therefore be about AD 62 or 63.

III. THE TEACHING OF COLOSSIANS

Since the Epistle is by way of a polemic against the false teaching it will be helpful to try and discover the type of error which was being propagated. Lightfoot argues very convincingly for its affinities with Essene Judaism, while Zahn[1] denies any connection between Essene teaching and the Colossian heresy. But it would seem to be of more importance to detect the elements in the false teaching as it actually was, than to demonstrate its spiritual ancestry. Even if Lightfoot is correct and the background is a Judaism of the Essene variety, it has

[1] T. Zahn, *Introduction to the New Testament*, p. 479.

clearly been modified by its contact with Greek thought. The main point, therefore, would seem to be the fact that the heresy appears as a blend of Jewish and Greek elements. In fact we seem to have a form of religious syncretism which was typical of the first century.

The influence of Greek philosophical thought is reflected in the underlying presupposition which clearly seems to be the antagonism between matter and spirit. The result of an acceptance of this antagonism is an attempt to conquer the body which is the prison-house of the soul. This attempt to deal with the body led in later Gnosticism to two completely opposite attitudes. On the one side there were those who sought to subdue the body by rigorous asceticism; and on the other there were those who claimed to hold the body in such contempt, since its activities had no influence on the soul, that licentious living was advocated. Here at Colossae there is no hint of an attack by Paul on libertinism, while he does attack the ascetic teaching, so that we may assume it was the latter which had been accepted. In the ascetic attempt to win fullness of salvation, Jewish law-keeping in terms of rigorous sabbath observance and abstaining from unclean meat (ii. 16) had their place. Indeed in view of Paul's words concerning the spiritual circumcision of Christ (ii. 11 ff., iv. 11) it is likely that the rite of physical circumcision was also enjoined as legally binding.

A further outcome of this philosophical dualism is an inevitable introduction of angelic beings who mediate between God and the world. Thus there arose a false humility in which a man professed to be utterly unworthy of approaching God and indeed unable to do so; and from this position followed the necessity of submission to the angelic powers and worship of the angels. In view of Paul's stress on Christ's work both in creation and redemption it would seem that the false teaching set these angelic powers forward as the agents through whom the world of matter came into being, and therefore the means whereby man might be redeemed from the bondage of material conditions and made free.

In the mystery cults which flourished in the apostolic age the great promise which was held out was salvation through enlightenment. Those who were initiated partook of the knowledge which was reserved for the inmost fellowship, and which was the means of deliverance. The rites and ceremonies of the cult were but the pathway to this esoteric knowledge. This element also is seen in the Colossian heresy if we notice Paul's insistence on the universality of the gospel, and also his stress on the true understanding and knowledge which are freely available through Christ, who is the source of wisdom and knowledge (i. 6, 25–28, ii. 2, 3).

The resultant religious amalgam is an attempt to advance beyond apostolic Christianity. There is no suggestion that Christ is openly rejected. He still has a place; but only as one among many angelic powers. Indeed Paul's emphasis on the primacy of Christ would suggest that the false teachers did not even put Him as *primus inter pares*. They do seem to admit that He has delivered His people from sin, but they still have to wage the battle against the cosmic powers; and in this they need, as we have seen, ascetic discipline, the help of the angelic powers, and initiation into the knowledge which brings not only enlightenment but also salvation.

It is difficult to say how far these various errors had been developed and to what extent they had been integrated into a system. Certainly there seems to be some specific body of wrong doctrine, for Paul seems to be dealing with one group of false teachers rather than with various groups holding differing views. Yet at the same time we must avoid the mistake of reading into the situation the clearly defined teaching of later Gnosticism. It is much more likely that we have here the beginning of what was later to be more clearly systematized. But Paul sees plainly that these tendencies are subversive of the gospel. His attack here was to be continued in the battles of the second century when Gnostic sects threatened to transform apostolic Christianity into something totally different.

Paul has one main answer to the erroneous teaching, and that is the Person and work of Christ; and so we get the high

Christology of the Epistle. In His Person Christ stands supreme and unique. He is no emanation of deity, for in Him the fullness of the Godhead dwells. He is the beloved Son. He is the image of the invisible God. Thus in virtue of His divine nature He is above and beyond every angelic power. But this superiority is seen also in His work. He is the One through whom the created order came into being. He is its sustainer and He is the very goal of its existence (i. 15-17). His relationship, not only to the world, but also to the angelic powers, is that of Creator to creature. Then again, in the work of redemption He has not left anything for either man or angel to accomplish, for His work is complete. He has satisfied the demands of the broken law and He has also won a complete victory over all the powers of evil. Thus His people do not need to try and keep the law as a means of justification, for He has met the law's demands (ii. 14). Nor do they need to try and fight against the cosmic powers, for He has already vanquished these (ii. 15).

But Christ has not done these mighty acts on behalf of His people while still remaining apart from them. They are His body (i. 18, 24), being in organic union with Him. Thus they were involved in His great redemptive acts. They died with Him and rose again with Him. Indeed their baptism is a vivid declaration of this fact. They are, then, no longer slaves in a hostile world from which they must free themselves by their own efforts. They have already been made free in virtue of their union with Christ, and it is for them to realize their status in actual experience. They do not need some higher teaching to achieve perfection, for in Christ they are complete.

IV. PHILEMON

The traditional view of the circumstances which gave birth to this letter is that Onesimus had been a slave of Philemon and had escaped to Rome, where he had come in contact with the apostle Paul and had been converted. The apostle wrote this letter urging his master to receive him back kindly and for Paul's sake (as it is to Paul that Philemon owes his own conversion), to receive this spiritual son of the apostle as a brother in Christ. Now certainly this view of the message of this brief letter would seem to be the plain meaning as we read it. It has however been called in question by Professor Knox who has suggested an alternative interpretation in his ingenious reconstruction of the story behind the Epistle.[1] We cannot lightly dismiss Knox's arguments which are brilliantly and persuasively presented. We must therefore examine them to see if they will sustain the conclusion to which they lead.

Knox begins with the obvious fact of the similarity of Colossians and Philemon. This is not only seen in the similar situation of the writer in each, but also in the fact that, as Knox sees it, the Colossian letter is overshadowed by Paul's concern over Onesimus. Thus the emphasis on 'bowels of mercies' in Colossians iii. 12 is paralleled by three references in Philemon: 7, 12, 20; and in addition, the strong word on the position of slaves in Colossians reflects the same influence at work in the apostle's mind. But then comes Knox's novel theory. It is Archippus not Philemon who is the owner of the slave; and it is in his house at Colossae that the church meets. Knox contends that there is no evidence in the letter to Philemon to prove that Philemon was the owner. Furthermore, says Knox, Paul was not sending Onesimus back to his master that he might remain there. He was rather sending a request that Onesimus might return to share with Paul his work in the gospel. Now the letter which he sends back with Onesimus is, Knox maintains, the letter 'from Laodicea' mentioned in Colossians iv. 16. This means that Philemon really lived at Laodicea and the letter went first to him to be despatched to Archippus in whose house the church at Colossae met. A further link in his argument is the call to Archippus to fulfil his ministry. Now this comes immediately after the mention of the letter from Laodicea, and would naturally fit in with the service Paul wishes him to render in the matter of Onesimus, assuming that he is the latter's owner. The final conjecture in the argument stems from the mention in the letter of Ignatius to the Ephesians, at the beginning of the second century,

[1] *Philemon among the Letters of Paul*, 1935.

of an Onesimus whom Knox claims to be the same man. The part this Onesimus played in collecting the Pauline letters in the canon would account for the inclusion of the apparently slight letter to Philemon, in which however he would obviously have a deep personal interest.

There are however some very strong objections which may be levelled against Knox's position and which make it completely untenable. The Epistle to Philemon is addressed primarily to Philemon and not to Archippus. Furthermore with this address to Philemon is the mention of the church 'in thy house'. Had the church been in Archippus' house, as Knox suggests, he would surely have written 'in his house'. This places Philemon in Colossae and not in Laodicea as Knox's theory would require. Furthermore, if Philemon occupied such a position of importance in the churches of the Lycus valley that a letter to Archippus in Colossae had to go via Philemon in Laodicea, it seems very strange that the major letter to the Colossians was not sent to the more important centre first. Then again Tychicus is not mentioned in Philemon. This is perfectly natural if, as we maintain, this letter was sent with Colossians, but not if it was going separately to Laodicea. Knox tries to extract himself from the difficulty by admitting that the letter was sent to Colossae, but that it went via Laodicea. But this fails to do justice to the request in Colossians iv. 16. There Paul envisages an exchange of letters which are to be read in the respective churches. But the letter is addressed not only to Philemon himself, but to the Colossian church which met at his house. It would be pointless then to give orders for the letter to be read publicly in Colossae, when the opening of the letter shows that it is not simply a personal note to Philemon, but is addressed also to the church. Furthermore, as C. F. D. Moule points out, it is a very inadequate view which would equate the ministry which Archippus is called on to discharge, as being simply the treatment of Onesimus. By its very description it suggests something which has been handed on to him, and so speaks rather of an office in the church which he is to fulfil.

As far as the mention of Onesimus in the Ignatian letter is concerned, we may be prepared to accept him as being the same person as the former slave of Philemon. But it would seem to be an unjustifiable conclusion to suggest that his personal interest secured the inclusion of Philemon in the canon—even assuming that he had a hand in the collection of the Pauline writings. The reason for such an inclusion is surely to be sought at a deeper level than one man's personal desire. Is the answer not partly in the fact already noted that this is not only a personal letter but also a letter to a church? Thus, while the bulk of the letter is in the second person singular, the opening and conclusion embrace the fellowship of which Philemon was a member. This suggests that the appeal to Philemon was not to be seen as a purely personal word to him; but had a message for the church as well. But in the providential ordering of the Holy Spirit, what was of concern to the local church, though it was rooted in an intensely personal matter, has, by the inclusion of the letter in the canon, brought its message to the whole Church of God.

V. SLAVERY

The particular issue with which Philemon deals, reflects the prevailing economic background of the Roman Empire. Slavery was a long-established institution and was accepted by all as a normal feature of the social structure. The treatment of slaves was on the whole callous. In some cases savage punishment was the result of the slightest mistake on their part. They were looked on as things, not as persons; and their master had absolute right over them. It is true that voices were raised, for example among the Stoics, calling for a more humane attitude, but they were a tiny minority. Speaking generally, the condition of the average slave was wretched beyond words.

It is all the more surprising that there is no condemnation of slavery as such in the New Testament. It is true, as we shall see, that it had something to say on the subject which meant a radical transformation of the attitude to be adopted to it;

but we never find any statement that slavery is intrinsically wrong. It is not enough to say in reply that slavery was so much a part of the social fabric that to attack it would have been revolutionary doctrine, which would have called forth the opposition of the authorities. The apostles were not governed by expediency, but by truth. After all, idolatry was also part of the social cement of life in the Roman Empire, yet they attacked it unsparingly; and indeed it was this very attack which was the reason for much of the hostility which they incurred. One can think of the fury of the crowd in Ephesus incited by Demetrius. He was obviously more concerned with his business than with his religion; but the ease with which the crowd was stirred shows how any attack on idolatry was a dangerous line to follow. Nor may we say that respect for the ruling authorities, which would prevent any recourse to physical attempts to overthrow the institution, necessarily implies an acceptance of it. It is true that passive submission would be a Christian virtue to be exercised in face of the provocation of servitude under a pagan master. But while a Christian slave might therefore be called to submit, such submission could be allied with an acknowledgment of the inherent evil of the condition of slavery. But nowhere is this acknowledgment found. Indeed, what is more striking is that when Paul appeals to Philemon as a Christian owner of a slave he never suggests that slavery *per se* is immoral. Yet surely this would have been natural, since he was dealing with a situation within a church fellowship, and was not preaching publicly in such a way as to inflame passions. The silence of the New Testament must therefore be explained on other grounds.

In view of all the callous brutality which has been associated with the practice all through the years, it becomes extremely difficult to see the institution apart from the savagery which has surrounded it. What then, stripped of its accompanying abuses, is the essential idea in slavery? It is surely the right of one man to share in the outcome of the labour of another, when the other man is forced to render it. Now there is nothing intrinsically immoral in sharing in the fruit of another man's

22

toil. After all, in the relation between a master and a free servant, when once the latter has accepted terms of service, the contract means a sharing of one in the fruit of the other's labour; and that labour must be rendered because of the terms already accepted. Thus, in the Old Testament, there is envisaged the possibility of the slave, who voluntarily continues as such, relinquishing his freedom and preferring to remain as the slave of a man he trusts and loves (Ex. xxi. 5; Dt. xv. 16). Further, if a man becomes indebted to another, there is no essential immorality in his repaying his debt by means of labour rendered. Yet this labour by its nature is something forced, which is of the essence of slavery.[1]

If, then, the New Testament writers did not attack the essential element of slavery, what did they say which revolutionized the thinking of the Christian on the subject? In the first place masters were taught that they had a responsibility towards their slaves. To us this seems an obvious truth; but it was far from obvious to the Roman world. A master had no obligations whatever to a slave, who was simply a living chattel in his household. Paul insists, however, 'Masters, give unto your servants that which is just and equal.' So the labour of the slave is to receive an adequate and fair reward. But if this is applied, it lifts his status to that of the free man who is under contract. It means that payment is not a mere pittance to keep the slave sufficiently healthy for further work. It means rather that he is to be recompensed in accordance with the service rendered, and this clearly involves food, clothing, and the ability to maintain a family life. This kind of slavery is far removed from the wretched servitude of the unfortunate serfs in the average pagan Roman household.

Then Paul teaches slaves that they are to regard themselves as persons. When he says 'Servants, obey in all things your masters', he is really taking a completely new attitude to slaves. To exhort someone to a course of action is to treat them as responsible moral beings. But this was precisely what had

[1] For a very able discussion of this difficult subject see John Murray, *Principles of Conduct*, 1957, pp. 93 ff.

not been done in the past; and the result must have been seen not only in the mind of the slave's owner but of the slave himself. Treat a man with a brutal disregard and he will lose all self-respect. He will become a servile cringing creature. He will cease to look on himself as a man. He will become brutalized. So Paul teaches the Christian slave a new self-respect. He is not like a beast of burden compelled by force to do a job. He is a child of God, conscious of his responsibility before God, and seeing even his condition as one where he can glorify his Saviour.

The final stage is reached in Philemon. Here the master – servant relationship is not denied; but it is caught up into a new relationship which transmutes the former. Onesimus is to be received no longer as a slave but as a brother. In Christ both master and servant stand together, for they are one in Him. When Paul urges Philemon to receive Onesimus as a beloved brother he has set the slave in a position where the legal title of slave ceases to be of primary importance.

COLOSSIANS: ANALYSIS

I. INTRODUCTION (i. 1–14).

    a. Salutation (i. 1, 2).
    b. Thanksgiving (i. 3–8).
    c. Paul's prayer for them (i. 9–14).

II. THE PERSON AND WORK OF CHRIST (i. 15–23).

    a. The pre-eminence of the Son (i. 15–20).
    b. God's purpose for the Colossians (i. 21–23).

III. PAUL'S PART IN GOD'S PLAN (i. 24–ii. 7).

    a. His sufferings (i. 24, 25).
    b. The mystery of Christ (i. 26–28).
    c. Paul's prayer for his readers (i. 29–ii. 5).
    d. A call to continuance (ii. 6, 7).

IV. WARNING AGAINST FALSE TEACHING (ii. 8–23).

    a. Philosophy and truth (ii. 8, 9).
    b. New men in Christ (ii. 10–15).
    c. Christian liberty (ii. 16–23).

V. A NEW PATTERN OF LIFE (iii. 1–iv. 1).

    a. New aims for new men (iii. 1–4).
    b. Mortifying the old nature (iii. 5–11).
    c. Putting on the new (iii. 12–17).
    d. Practical injunctions (iii. 18–iv. 1).

VI. FINAL INSTRUCTIONS (iv. 2–6).

    a. The duty of prayer (iv. 2–4).
    b. The duty of witness (iv. 5, 6).

VII. PERSONAL GREETINGS (iv. 7–18).

COLOSSIANS: COMMENTARY

I. INTRODUCTION (i. 1-14)

a. Salutation (i. 1, 2)

1. Paul stresses the authority with which he speaks by describing himself as *an apostle of Jesus Christ*. The apostle in the New Testament is not merely an emissary. He is rather 'one clothed with the authority and endued with the power of the Sender'.[1] It is significant, as Lightfoot points out in his comment on Philippians i[2] that, while Paul asserts his apostolic commission in writing to those churches where it was necessary to assert his authority, he omits mention of it in his letters to the Philippians and Thessalonians who were obviously linked to him by a warm bond of friendship and loyalty. Similarly, in the personal letter to Philemon where he is asking a favour he does not use his title. By contrast, the letter to the Galatian churches, where his authority was challenged, has a very strong assertion of his apostolic position. In writing to the Colossians he does not need to stress it so strongly, yet it is clearly affirmed since his readers, who do not know him personally, must understand that he speaks by command of Christ. Thus his words are more than the opinion of the great missionary of the early Church; they are rather the authoritative utterance of the divinely appointed mouthpiece of Christ. When the Colossians read this word of Paul, they must receive it not as from Paul the man, but from Paul the apostle, and so as the word of God. This emphasis on his apostolic status and authority is brought out further by his description of Timothy. He associates the latter with him in the letter; but while Paul is *an apostle* Timothy is still only the *brother* (see

[1] Norval Geldenhuys, *Supreme Authority*, 1953, p. 63. This book gives an excellent treatment of the New Testament conception of the apostolate. See pp. 46 ff.

[2] Commentary, p. 25.

RV mg.; cf. Rom. xvi. 23; 1 Cor. i. 1; 1 Cor. xvi. 12). This high calling is not due to any innate ability in Paul, nor to his undoubted intellectual attainments. It is due to the grace and mercy of the God who has chosen him—it is *by the will of God* that he is 'an apostle of Christ Jesus'. The order of words in this latter title (see RV) suggests a stress on the word *Christ*. H. C. G. Moule sees this as a reflection of the messianic glory of the Saviour. Certainly this usage, which is frequent with Paul, would be quite in line with his lofty conception of the glory of the Saviour; and in this Epistle would be specially apt in view of his extended treatment of the pre-eminence of Christ.

2. The letter is addressed *to the saints* in *Colosse* and to the *faithful brethren in Christ*. In the order of words in the Greek the phrase *in Colosse* appears prominently at the beginning of the sentence. Thus there is the vivid contrast between the description of the readers as saints and their present situation. They are in Colossae, a small insignificant town overshadowed by its rich neighbours Laodicea and Hierapolis. Hence they are prone to the provincialism, pettiness, and lack of vision of a small community. Further, they are in Colossae with all its paganism and idolatry. For them, as a minority group, there will constantly be the temptation to give way to social pressure and so to compromise their witness. But they must recall that they are *saints*. This title speaks of their status, rather than of the actual degree of holiness attained. As Lightfoot points out on Philippians i. 1, it is a word with an Old Testament background. The Old Testament Israel was a people apart. They were saints because they were marked off from the nations around and consecrated to God. Indeed it was because of their exalted status that the prophets demanded so much of them in terms of actual holiness. These Christians in Colossae must remember too, amid all the temptations to stagnation or to compromise, that they are likewise men with a high calling. They may live in a small Asiatic town but they do so as the people of God.

The phrase that follows, describing them further as the

faithful brethren in Christ, serves as an amplification. Lightfoot suggests that Paul is here hinting indirectly at the defection in the Colossian church by addressing himself specifically to the brethren who have remained faithful. While this is attractive, it hardly seems possible in view of the similar opening in the Epistle to the Ephesians. In that letter Paul is not going to develop a controversial theme, and yet he writes 'to the faithful'. It would seem best to regard the phrase as bringing a stimulus and an encouragement. It stimulates them by calling those who are set apart for God to be faithful to their high calling. It encourages them by reminding them that they are not alone in Colossae. As saints unto God they are also brethren of all the people of God. Indeed the use of the word *brethren* so soon after the description of Timothy as 'our brother' suggests such a unity. But even this sense of fellowship with the whole people of God is not Paul's final word about their status. What gives them their highest assurance is their relationship to Christ. While it is true that a realization of Christian fellowship is a help and encouragement to those who witness in Colossae, yet ultimately both they and their brethren stand because they are *in Christ*.

The familiar greeting which opens nearly all Paul's letters is here shortened. It is better with the RV to omit the phrase *and the Lord Jesus Christ* which is an addition in the Received Text, and so appears in the AV. It can easily be understood how this phrase was added in many manuscripts because of the scribes' desire to make the greeting conform to the usual pattern. This tendency may be seen in 1 Thessalonians (see RV) where the greeting is even shorter, but where many copyists have again expanded it to the full Pauline greeting of the other Epistles.

The word *grace*, *charis*, has a wealth of meaning drawn not merely from its original Greek usage, but also from its Old Testament associations. These are further developed and enriched by the fuller content poured into the word by the New Testament writers.[1] The LXX has used it to translate the

---

[1] J. Armitage Robinson, *St. Paul's Epistle to the Ephesians*, 1941, pp. 221 ff.

Hebrew word *chēn* which speaks of the blessedness enjoyed by one who is favoured by a superior. Thus *charis* spoke of the favour of God, and of the blessedness of the life so favoured by the Lord. Paul with his Old Testament background takes this conception and makes it even richer. Grace is freely bestowed by God apart from man's deserving. Thus the use of the word in the salutation is much more than a mere greeting. It is a prayer that they may enjoy the blessing of God Himself. Hence it is very appropriate that the prayer for *grace* should be linked to that for *peace*. *Eirēnē*, which translates the Old Testament word *shalōm*, speaks of the healthy condition of the life experienced by the man who enjoys God's favour. Indeed the phrase is immeasurably enriched by the fact that *grace* and *peace* flow from the God whose relationship to us is in terms of the title bestowed by Christ: *our Father*. Instead of the inner discord which is an inevitable result of sin, the recipient of the free grace of God enjoys an inner harmony, even in the midst of the spiritual conflict which the Christian constantly wages.

b. Thanksgiving (i. 3–8)

3. There is a ring of sincerity about Paul's thanksgiving as he writes to the various churches. Thus in the Epistle to the Galatians and in 2 Corinthians he omits it, showing that he only included it when he really believed it was due. Further, his commendation of these Colossians is raised above the level of flattery, or even of congratulation, by the form in which he casts it. It was true that they had exhibited faith in Christ, and love to all the saints; but Paul is too keenly aware that honour and glory are due to God alone to congratulate them. Rather must he give all the glory to God; and so his commendation is transformed into a prayer of thanks to the God who is ultimately responsible for any spiritual advance in His children. In a day when Christians too easily slip into the worldly attitude of glorifying men, even though they be godly men, here is a salutary reminder of a basic principle of Scripture: 'My glory will I not give to another.' (See Is. xlii. 8, xlviii. 11.)

It is probably best with RV and RSV to omit *and*. This would mean that the genitive *our Lord Jesus Christ* is governed by the word *Father* only and not also by *God*, as in Ephesians i. 3, 17. It may be that Paul, dealing with the Colossians, will not offer them even the slightest opportunity of misconstruing his meaning and giving the Lord Jesus Christ a subordinate place. God the Father and the Lord Jesus Christ share the same divine nature.

Paul's thanksgiving is not merely a temporary feeling of gratitude which comes to him as he pens this letter. It is a constant experience. Indeed it is a prime element in all his prayers for them, if the words *praying always for you* are linked with the preceding sentence. Even in such an apparently incidental way we find a frequent note of Paul's teaching, that true prayer is not only in terms of petition, but should always be in the context of thanksgiving to God (Phil. iv. 6; Col. iv. 2; 1 Thes. v. 17, 18; 1 Tim. ii. 1).

4. What calls for thanksgiving is, in the first place, their faith. The phrase *in Christ Jesus* does not mean in this context that Christ is the object of their faith, though this is of course true, for in that case the prepositions *eis* or *epi* would be required. It is rather Paul's familiar usage which we have seen already in verse 2. They are *in Christ* in the sense of drawing their life from Him. He is the sphere in which they move. All that they have, or hope to be, is due to their intimate relationship with Him. Thus the faith which they exhibit draws its vitality from their link with Christ. The exercise of that faith is controlled by their union with Him. Hence the whole Godward aspect of their life which is covered by the word *faith*, is dominated by Christ.

It is inevitable that where such healthy faith is present there must also be a true *love* for the brethren. The primacy of faith for the Christian does not lead to a solitary or exclusive piety. It is his very concentration on God which purges him of his selfishness, and gives him a new perspective in his relationship with others. Because of his faith in the Father his heart goes out to all those who share with him this high experience of sonship. Such Christian love is but a reflection of the love which God has towards us. It is significant too that such love is directed towards *all the saints*, not to those of the same social class or intellectual stratum. It is to all the saints without exception that true Christian love is shown. The communion of saints means, not a series of loosely related cliques, but an all-embracing and self-abnegating fellowship.

5. It seems best to read with RV 'because of'. This would link the mention of *hope*, not with the giving of thanks, but with *faith* and *love*. Not only does it stand closer grammatically to these, but in Paul's mind the three are closely linked, as in 1 Corinthians xiii. 13. Thus the implication is that the Christian's hope is the motive power behind his faith and his love. Indeed, as Paul points out in 1 Corinthians xv. 12 ff., if the Christian life is in terms of this world only, then faith is a mockery and morality a waste of time. The only logical outcome of a life which is not dominated by the Christian hope is 'let us eat and drink; for tomorrow we die'. But in fact the Christian has a sure hope; and so he does not live for himself, but as one who has an eternal destiny, he seeks to develop his faith and his love.

Hope may be used in the objective sense of something given, or in the subjective sense of the inward response of the heart to the promise. Here it is used primarily in its objective sense. The faith and love of the Colossians have been nourished, not by an inner effort of the will, but rather by the solid fact of the promises of God. This hope of the coming of the Saviour, of the resurrection of the body and of life everlasting, is something given by God. As such it depends, not on whether they can maintain a mood of optimism in changing circumstances, but on the unchanging character of God. Thus it is described as being *laid up* for them *in heaven*. The same word *apokeimai* is used in the parable of the talents to describe the one talent kept securely in a napkin (Lk. xix. 20). So the hope of glory is carefully kept by God as a treasure which one day they will fully share.

The means whereby this objective hope becomes an inner experience is through the hearing of the gospel. Just as 'faith cometh by hearing, and hearing by the word of God' (Rom. x. 17), so, too, hope is not the product of a fertile imagination, but comes and develops through a study of the word of the gospel. The term *word*, *logos*, means both reason and word, and may refer both to the process of thought and to the word which expresses the thought. Hence the word of the gospel is the outward revelation by God, in the apostolic message, of His purpose of blessing for men. The emphasis is that behind the gospel is the revealing act of God, who is thus at once the Author of redemption and the source of the Christian hope.

The phrase *the truth of the gospel* may be taken in either of two ways. It may refer to the truth which is contained in the message of the gospel. Thus the 'word . . . of the gospel' means the declaration of the truth of God embodied in the apostolic message. Or, it may refer to the gospel in its integrity, the true gospel in contrast with false teaching. This seems the more likely interpretation if we compare Galatians ii. 5, 14. The thought then would be that the Colossians had heard the word beforehand, *proēkousate*, in the preaching of the apostolic message in its purity and integrity, before erroneous teachers had begun to substitute another gospel. It is the word given in the true gospel which is the source of hope. Once let the grasp on that gospel grow slack, or once permit that truth to be adulterated, and the Christian hope will grow correspondingly dim.

6. This gospel has come to the Colossians, not merely in the sense of being brought by men, but in the deeper sense of being a message from God. The gospel is not something that men reach by a growth in religious development or perception. It is essentially a message that comes from above as a word revealed from God. The theme of the gospel is *the grace of God*, who has taken the initiative and come to meet and to save men. In contrast with false teaching which speaks in terms of legalism (ii. 14–21) the true gospel declares what God has done for men. Hence, involved in the coming of the gospel is a personal coming to them of God Himself.

Nor must they think that this gospel is just one more competitor among the mystery religions of the Roman Empire. It is not merely an addition to the local religous cults of the cities of Asia Minor. It is rather a message for the whole world; and its diffusion in the Empire is indicative of its world-wide scope. But while regarding the gospel as a message for the whole world, they must keep the balance by seeing not only its universal, but also its individual application. Thus Paul parallels the coming of the word *in all the world* with its coming among them (*kathōs kai en panti tō kosmō . . . kathōs kai en humin*). Let them then maintain both truths. Let them hold on to the individual aspect of the coming of the gospel, and they will avoid the religious vagueness which fails to see the need for a personal meeting with God. Let them hold on to the universal aspect, and they will avoid the tendency to defeatism to which a religious minority is so prone.

The two characteristics of the true gospel are its fruitfulness and its growth (the MS evidence is all in favour of adding 'growing' which is omitted in the Received Text and in the AV). It is because of its divine origin that it is fruitful. The merely human word at best lingers in the memory as a stimulus. But this word, because it is God's word, is living; and so it has the inherent power of bearing *fruit* when it falls into the divinely-prepared soil of a receptive heart. This fruitfulness is seen in two directions: first in the reconciliation of a man to God, when he is justified by faith in the Christ whom the gospel declares; and secondly in the actual transforming of his character by the Holy Spirit, who uses the word of God as the means of sanctification. But the gospel not only works deeply within but it is constantly growing in influence. In the providence of God these two are linked. It is normally through its fruitfulness in the individual that it reaches out through him to others; and so depth of holiness is matched by a growth in the impact of the gospel upon other lives.

The message of *the grace of God* came to the Colossians in

B   33

true and undiluted form. They made it their own as they heard, and then grasped, with a spiritual apprehension, the significance of the facts preached to them. The reception of the gospel is never a mere emotional reaction, nor is it only intellectual assent. True, it begins with hearing the word of truth; but allied to hearing there must be the understanding which comes as a result of the illumination of the Holy Spirit. Paul uses the word understanding, *epignōsis*, more frequently in his later Epistles (see Lightfoot p. 135 and also on Phil. i. 9). It has the intensive meaning involved in the prefix *epi*, and speaks of knowledge which is much deeper than mere mental grasp. The use of the cognate verb here (*knew*) implies an assimilation of the inner meaning of the gospel, so that truth is transformed into experience. Such a deepening grasp of the gospel is a prerequisite to knowing its fruitfulness and power.

7. The weight of the manuscript evidence is in favour of reading 'for us' rather than *for you*. This also gives a better meaning. *Epaphras* was the bearer of the good news. But his mission was no mere individual enterprise, for he went with the full support of Paul. Indeed he preached on Paul's behalf ('for us'). Here is the first hint in the Epistle that Paul has not actually visited Colossae himself (see also ii. 1). But above and beyond the commission of the apostle is the authority of Christ. Epaphras may have been sent by Paul; but ultimately he was the *minister of Christ*.

8. Epaphras not only carried the gospel to Colossae, but also brought back to Paul a report of the way in which the message had borne fruit in human lives. There had been the growth of that characteristic Christian grace, *agapē*, or *love*. This love has a twofold aspect as it is directed first towards God and then towards men (see verse 4 above). It is not to be equated with ordinary human love, *erōs*, but is rather a supernatural grace bestowed and maintained by the Holy Spirit.

c. Paul's prayer for them (i. 9–14)

9. Knowledge of the growth in grace of our fellow Christians should never lead to any slackening of desire on our part that they might continue to progress. Indeed, by his introductory phrase *for this cause . . . also*, Paul emphasizes that it is the very facts which have given such cause for thanksgiving which are also an incentive to continue in unceasing prayer for them. His prime request is that they may be *filled with the knowledge* (*epignōsis*) of God's *will*. It is significant that knowledge of the will of God is looked on as preceding a life that is pleasing to Him. The word *filled*, *plēroō*, suggests the idea of filling out to completeness. Hence the thought is that the imperfection and inadequacy of our knowledge of God's will must be more and more corrected by our growth in a deeper understanding (see verse 6, *epignōsis*). Such knowledge is not the product of the fleshly wisdom of the world which puffs up but does not enlighten the inner man (cf. 1 Cor. i. 20, ii. 5, 6, 13, iii. 19). It comes rather from the illumination of the Holy Spirit. He it is who gives that *wisdom* and *understanding* which enables us to know the will of God. *Wisdom* speaks of that settled condition of the mind whose thinking is not dependent merely on the unaided processes of the human intellect, but is controlled and enlightened by the Spirit of truth. *Understanding, sunesis,* speaks of the application of this basic wisdom to the various problems which present themselves to us and require a clear analysis before a decision can be taken (see note in Lightfoot here and on Eph. i. 18).

10. The Colossians must not, however, be misled into thinking that their goal is a barren orthodoxy. Hellenistic Judaism may content itself with an intellectual growth in religious knowledge divorced from life; but *the knowledge of God* to which the Christian aspires will reveal itself in transformation of character. So Paul continues to pray, not that they may be moulded to the conventional moral pattern of the community; nor that they may make their own capabilities the standard of conduct; but rather that they may aim to *walk* *worthy of the Lord* Himself. Nothing less than the holiness and love of the Son of God must be their aim. And in their constant striving towards this high goal they should rise above the mere desire to succeed because of the satisfaction this brings. They must rather have a God-centred motive, and live entirely with a view to pleasing Him. The addition of the epithet *all* qualifying *pleasing* suggests further that they are not to be limited by consideration of their duty, but are to aim at complete, or whole-hearted, pleasing of God. *Areskeia, pleasing,* originally referred to the cringing attitude before a patron; but such an attitude assumes a very different character when it is adopted before God. He is the Creator, while we are but creatures of the dust. He is Almighty, and we are puny sinful men. Before Him we do well to bow in utter submission. To please Him in all things must be our highest desire.

The life that is lived with such a controlling purpose will naturally manifest itself in active endeavour. Its fruitfulness will be far-reaching and pervasive. We are taking the two participles *being fruitful* and *increasing* as both referring to *every good work*. What sustains this increasing fruitfulness is *the knowledge of God*. If we follow the likely reading *tē epignosei*, rather than *en epignosei* or *eis epignosin* (AV and RV), we may interpret in two ways. H. C. G. Moule suggests that it is a dative of reference and means that we are to increase with regard to the knowledge of God. But this is virtually a repetition of the request earlier that we might be filled with this knowledge. Lightfoot's suggestion seems more to the point. He translates it 'by the knowledge of God' (cf. RV mg.). This avoids the repetition, and yet underlines again what Paul has already emphasized in his prayer, namely that knowledge of the will of God is basic to any spiritual or moral growth.

11. A second characteristic of this God-centred life is its source of power. While the apostle prays that they may live a life pleasing to God, it is with this complementary thought in mind, that they may know the strengthening of God for such a life. There seems to be a parallel between 'in every good work' (*en panti ergō agathō*) and *with all might* (*en pasē dunamei*). This suggests that for every requirement there is power available. No matter how wide the demand of Christian service may be, nor how difficult by human standards, there are always available divine resources to match it. Further, it is significant that this receiving of power is a continuous experience. *Strengthened* translates the continuous present participle *dunamoumenoi*. The Christian does not receive an initial impetus which must serve him for the whole journey. He may confidently expect that the God who came to him in regenerating power will continue to strengthen him.

But while it is true that there is power available for every situation, it is not circumstances which finally determine the power of God. The phrase *according to his glorious power* suggests that the ultimate pledge of our being strengthened is the power inherent in God Himself. Our resources are not at the mercy of the exigencies of the moment, but are to be measured by the might of God. The glory of God speaks of the manifestation to men of His essential being. It is, as it were, the shining forth of His majesty. Thus the 'power of his glory' means the power which is declared to us when God reveals Himself. The word used for power, *kratos*, is in the New Testament used only of God. This essential divine power, when manifested to us, becomes in us *dunamis*, here translated *strength*, which energizes us and enables us to live lives that will please Him.

The threefold fruit of this strengthening is *patience, longsuffering*, and *joyfulness*. *Patience, hupomonē*, is that quality of steady persistence whereby a man continues to his goal. Thus it is used in Hebrews xii. 1 of the athlete who runs with dogged persistence the full course. It is not therefore so much a passive acceptance of the inevitable, as an active unrelenting endeavour even in spite of difficulty and trial. *Longsuffering, makrothumia*, is that virtue which is seen in face of provocation. Whereas the natural instinct is to retaliate, whether by bitter word or by an act of revenge, the Christian is to aim rather at that quiet

37

spirit which was exemplified by Him who in the moment of supreme provocation prayed 'Father, forgive them; for they know not what they do'. The third word in the triad is the characteristic word *joyfulness*. The Christian does not face difficulty and persecution with the stolid impassivity of the Stoic. His persistence and longsuffering are infused with joy. He rejoices because the goal of his persistence is Christ Himself. He rejoices that in quietly accepting the persecution of men he enters into a new fellowship with his Master.

Abbott argues with others that *with joyfulness, meta charas*, should be taken with the clause that follows. He contends as against Lightfoot that *eucharisteō* (to give thanks) does not necessarily imply joy, and may therefore be quite legitimately amplified by the preceding phrase. In favour of Lightfoot's position is the fact that Paul uses virtually the same phrase three times in the Epistle, and in the other two cases *eucharisteō* stands alone (i. 3, iii. 17). This reinforces his view that joyfulness is implicit in thanksgiving, and so it would be unnecessary to introduce such a phrase as *meta charas* especially in such an emphatic position. Olshausen goes further and suggests that *hupomonē* and *makrothumia* require the phrase *meta charas* in order to give them a truly Christian connotation. This contention cannot, however, be sustained in view of the fact that in the New Testament these words frequently stand alone. We may go so far with him as to say that the phrase here does fill out the words with meaning, without committing ourselves completely to his unjustified assertion.

12. There are two variant readings in this verse. The first one involves the words *tō hikanōsanti* (*hath made . . . meet*). A number of MSS read *tō kalesanti* (hath called) while one major MS (B) combines both. The similarity of the two readings easily accounts for the confusion. The weight of MS evidence, and also the more unfamiliar word (*hikanoō*) in this context, point to this as being the correct one. It is more difficult to decide between *us, hēmas*, and 'you', *humas*. There is strong MS evidence on both sides. Internal evidence would point in favour of *hēmas* (though Abbott takes the opposite view!) as it then runs parallel with the *hēmas* of the following clause. It is quite normal for Paul to switch in this way from the second person to the first in which he is including himself.

Paul has spoken of fruitfulness and power as two of the characteristics of the experience which he prays may be theirs; and now he turns to the third one, namely thanksgiving. The basic reason for this thanksgiving is our new status as Christians. This new status is emphasized in different ways. God is referred to absolutely as *the Father*. We had stood before the eternal Judge as guilty sinners condemned by the inexorable outworking of the law of holiness. But by the grace of God we have been adopted into the family, so that by faith and with confidence we can call the Judge 'our Father'. Again, our new position is illustrated against an Old Testament background. When the tribes entered Canaan they received the portion of their inheritance. We have been brought through Christ into a spiritual Canaan, into the light of fellowship with God. Already we are rich in God's gifts to us and we look forward to the perfection of our inheritance. This entry has not been due to our merits, but because God for Christ's sake has given us a title (*hikanoō*). Having thus been qualified by the gracious decree of God (note the aorist) we have been introduced into our inheritance which we share with the rest of the people of God, for *the saints*, or 'the separated ones', are now the Israel of God. Just as each tribe entered into the portion of land allotted to them so we enter into the sphere of blessing among the people of God which has been granted to us.

13. But behind this entry into our inheritance there was the prior deliverance. We were liberated from bondage and led into the land of liberty. Before our deliverance we were under *the power of darkness*. Sin held sway over us. The word *exousia, power*, is normally used in the New Testament in the straightforward sense of authority exercised over someone. Lightfoot's attempt to interpret it in the sense of arbitrary power, or tyranny, hardly seems to be supported by New Testament usage. In fact, with the background of Romans vi. we might say that in Paul's view sin has a legal authority over those who, as law-breakers, have become slaves of sin. It is because Christ has accepted the penalty of the broken law, having died to sin, that God may without injustice deliver us from the authority of sin.

The realm in which we were slaves is described as *darkness*. This implies not only absence of light, but opposition to the light. It is not only a condition of being without God, but of being against God. Hence we have been delivered from a rebel kingdom, and brought under the sovereignty of our rightful King. Just as a conqueror in the ancient world often transplanted an entire people to a new land, so our heavenly Conqueror has uprooted the people of God from alien soil and brought them to the liberty of their true homeland.

The phrase *his dear Son* is literally 'the Son of His love'. This is a richer expression than would be the case if the epithet beloved, *agapētos*, were used. The Son who is the only-begotten of the Father is not only the eternal object of the Father's love, but is also the embodiment and expression of that love in His gracious dealings with men. Thus to be translated into the kingdom of His Son is to move from the loveless condition of darkness and death into a spiritual realm in which we have the love of God shed upon us. As a result our relationship to our King and also to our fellow citizens is moulded by His love.

14. In Christ we have this deliverance. It is not merely that He is the agent, but it is through union with Him that we are redeemed. The word *apolutrōsis*, translated *redemption*, has its roots in the Old Testament. There the verb *lutrousthai* is frequently used to speak of the emancipation of the people of God from Egypt. Armitage Robinson, commenting on the similar verse, Ephesians i. 7, goes on to assert that in the New Testament usage of *apolutrōsis* and even of *lutrōsis*, 'the idea of emancipation is dominant and that of payment seems wholly to have disappeared'. But this can hardly be sustained in face of the constant New Testament emphasis on the cost of our deliverance. This is specifically stated by Christ in Mark x. 45 where He declares that He came 'to give his life a ransom (*lutron*) for many'. Again in 1 Timothy ii. 6 Christ is said to have given Himself 'a ransom (*antilutron*) for all'. The verb appears again in 1 Peter i. 18, 19 'ye were . . . redeemed . . . with the precious blood of Christ'; and so we might multiply examples. It is abundantly clear that deliverance is intimately linked with the price paid, and this price is nothing less than the death of Christ.[1]

We may omit the words *through his blood* as being an interpolation from Ephesians i. 7 for the ms attestation here is very weak. A more difficult question is whether we should read *we have*, *echomen*, or 'we had', *eschomen*. Lightfoot prefers the latter, and suggests that the similar variant in Ephesians i. 7 is due to an attempt to harmonize with the Colossian reading. In favour of Lightfoot is the fact that it follows three aorists (*hikanōsanti*, *errusato*, *metestēsen*). Abbott, however, maintains that it is unlikely that Paul would have used different tenses in two such similar verses; and also asserts that if the past were required a perfect would be more appropriate, as in Romans v. 2. The difference in exegesis would in any case be merely one of emphasis, whether on the fact that in Christ's death we were once and for all redeemed, or that in Him we now have redemption as a present possession.

Redemption is explained as involving *the forgiveness of sins*. The word *forgiveness*, *aphesis*, is infrequent with Paul, and does not appear in the LXX with this meaning. It does however appear (e.g. in Lv. xxv. 31) to describe the year of jubilee as being the year of release. To forgive is thus to release a man from the debt which he owes to God. His sin, which here is spoken of in terms of coming short of God's demands (*hamartia*), has put him hopelessly in debt to God's righteous justice. Forgiveness thus involves the remission of the penalty, freely given through Christ.

[1] See Leon Morris, *The Apostolic Preaching of the Cross*, 1955, pp. 9 ff.

II. THE PERSON AND WORK OF CHRIST (i. 15-23)

a. The pre-eminence of the Son (i. 15-20)

15, 16. Although we are introducing a fresh section here it is good to realize that this is largely for purposes of study, for there is no break in Paul's thought; and he continues with a relative pronoun, passing thus naturally from the fact of redemption to the glory of the Redeemer. The Son is the only perfect representation of God. Men may make images of God, but in so doing they deface the glory of the incorruptible God, as Paul shows in Romans i. 23. But in Christ, God's glory is not defaced but perfectly seen. Just as the image on the coin is a true copy of the head of the sovereign, or just as a child shows a marked likeness to a parent, so Christ in a deeper way is the perfect revelation to men of the invisible God. It is true that the phrase *the image of God* does not essentially involve the idea of perfection, for it is used of man in 1 Corinthians xi. 7. But here it must be interpreted against the background of the whole context in which the unique revelation of God given by the Son is clearly and fully declared. God dwells in light inaccessible, and may not be seen by human eyes, but in the Son we may see His true likeness.

He is supreme, first of all, in creation, being described as 'the firstborn of all creation' (RV). This must not be twisted, as it often has been, to mean that Christ stands at the apex of creation, but is still a created being. On purely grammatical grounds it would be possible to take the phrase with this meaning. Thus 'all creation' would be the totality of which the Son is the firstborn, and the genitive would then be partitive or qualifying. But the context rules this out completely. We must therefore take the genitive as being qualified by the element 'first' in the compound 'firstborn'. This then underlines the Son's primacy. He is begotten of the Father, not created; and as *firstborn, prōtotokos*, He is before all creation. Lightfoot, in an extended note, emphasizes that here it is the Son in His eternal being who is being described, rather than the Son as incarnate. In fact, there is a close parallel between this passage and John's teaching concerning the eternal Word or *Logos*. The only-begotten is also the agent of creation. The phrase 'in Christ' is often used in relation to salvation as meaning that union with Christ is vital. So here AV *by him* is used of creation in the sense that He is the agent by whom creation came into being.

Lest there should be any doubt as to the superiority of the Son to other spiritual beings, Paul stresses that He is not only the agent of the creation of the visible world, but also of the invisible world of heavenly beings. These beings who comprise both the angels of God and also the devil and his angels—Paul uses synonymous terms here without giving a precise classification—are all alike due to the creative power of the Son, and so are subject to His control. In fact He is not only the agent, but the very goal of their creation. They exist with a view to His glory, and so are subservient to His eternal purpose.

17. Far from being in any way a part of creation, the Son is *before all things*, not only in the sense that He is eternal, while creation is in time; but also in the sense that His very being, as the only-begotten of the Father, raises Him to a unique position above and before all that is due to the creative act of God. Indeed He is not only the agent of creation, but of preservation. The philosopher may seek for a principle of coherence, a unity amid all the diversity of the world of sense; but in the Son the believer finds the true principle of coherence. It is His power alone which holds creation together.

18. But the same One who is Lord of Creation is also Lord of the Church. Paul here passes almost imperceptibly from dealing with the Son in His eternal being to the incarnate One in His present glorified state. When dealing with His relation to creation he moves in the realm of the Son's past accomplishment or of His essential being. But here, while it is true that he stresses the Son's present Lordship in His Church, he also speaks of His becoming, *genētai*, pre-eminent through the triumph of the resurrection.

He is *the head of the body, the church*. Here we have a picture of Christ's relationship to His Church already made familiar by Paul's usage in 1 Corinthians xii. 12 and Romans xii. 5. As Head of the Church He is in an organic relationship, for the Church shares His very life, just as the limbs share a common life with the head. He is, further, the directing and controlling power to which the limbs must submit. Indeed that which gives them their unity as a body, and enables them to function purposefully, is the control of the Head. So true unity and effective endeavour in the body of Christ are due, not to a reorganization of the members, but to a renewed obedience to the divine Head.

He is *the beginning* in relation to the Church. This refers not only to His being first in time, but also to His being the very fount of the Church's life. The word *beginning* is associated closely with creation both in Genesis i. 1 and in John i. 1–3. So in the new spiritual creation the Lord is still the beginning, the source of life. The word is amplified by the phrase which follows—*the firstborn from the dead*. It is His resurrection, the emergence of life victorious over death, which establishes His title to be the source of life. But since He was the first to be so raised, the resurrection also established His primacy over those who should experience a like resurrection. There is no contradiction here involved in stating that He is the 'firstborn from the dead', and in accepting the raising of Lazarus or any other such miracles in Scripture. Lazarus was raised to his former corruptible condition, and was still liable to death; but the Son was raised incorruptible, never to taste death again.

The purpose of God is that the Son who is eternally supreme may, in the realm of time and in the sphere of revelation, become pre-eminent. This pre-eminence is to be as wide in scope as it is possible to be. He is to be supreme in all respects, and at every point. Lord of creation and Lord of His Church, He must be Lord in the lives of His own, with a sovereignty which brooks no rival.

19. It is extremely difficult to decide in what way we should

44

take this verse grammatically. The AV supplies the words *the Father* while the RSV takes 'the fulness' as the subject. The latter is quite legitimate from the purely grammatical point of view, and Abbott argues strongly in favour of this position. But his arguments founder on the rock of the following sentence. If we take 'the fulness' as the subject we are forced to take it as the subject of 'to reconcile' in verse 20. But to speak of the fullness of God being pleased to reconcile all things is to deal with an abstraction that sounds alien to anyone accustomed to Paul's normal mode of thinking, in which God personally is the author of reconciliation. It seems best then to follow Lightfoot and to supply the word 'God' as subject—which is virtually the position of the AV. We then have the characteristic biblical note that the Son's unique status is due to the eternal purpose of God. He is the beloved Son in whom the Father is well pleased.

The *for* which begins the verse points to what has preceded. The Son is supreme in Creation and in the Church; it is the eternal plan of God that in Him all the fullness should dwell. His supremacy stems from the fact that the incarnate Son is fully divine; and this unique divine-human person is the visible expression of the good pleasure of God.

The word *fulness* is rich in content; and Lightfoot has an extended note on it,[1] with which we might compare Armitage Robinson's.[2] If we take the verb to fill (*plēroō*) in its derived sense—and this is a frequent usage—as meaning to complete or to fulfil, the *fulness* then means the completion or the totality. It is used in classical Greek of the complement of a ship or the population of a city, signifying that number which makes the group complete. In the Gospels it is used of the filling up of the hole by the patch. Paul uses it in Romans xiii. 10 of the fulfilling or completing of the law. The meaning thus oscillates between a passive and an active sense; but the main idea is of completeness or totality. So here Paul is insisting, possibly or probably in face of false teaching, that in Christ the completeness of deity dwells. He is not merely endued in an especial

[1] *Op. cit.*, p. 255. [2] *Commentary on Ephesians*, p. 255.

45

way with the Holy Spirit, but is rather the dwelling-place of the very essence of God.

The word used here for dwelling, *katoikeō*, speaks of taking up residence. It does not necessarily involve permanent residence, as Lightfoot suggests, as we may see from Acts ii. 5 and vii. 4. It acquires the content of permanence when it is contrasted with the similar word *paroikeō* as in Genesis xxxvi. 44 (LXX).[1] Nor can we draw from it, as Olshausen does, an allusion to the Shekinah, because in the LXX *katoikeō* is not normally used in this context. It seems best therefore not to attempt to read into the word more than is there, and simply to take it as expressing the truth that the fullness of God has its residence or dwelling-place in the Son.

20. The good pleasure of the Father is seen further in the reconciliation effected through the Son. This truth follows from the foregoing; for it is because the Son is the dwelling-place of the fullness of God, that He is able to be the agent of atonement. This reconciliation was a decisive act (note the aorist tense), and there was a once-for-all element too about the making of *peace* which God effected. This was accomplished by *the blood of his cross*. This speaks first of the death of Christ in terms of a violent end. His death was due to the shedding of His blood. But blood speaks also of a sacrifice offered and so we have the thought that the sacrificial death of Christ is the means of reconciliation. But further, it is blood shed on a cross; and for Paul the cross was the place of one under a curse (see Gal. iii. 13 ff.). Here we are at the heart of the apostolic message of the cross, that Christ by the offering of Himself through death accepted the curse which was due to us. Thus His death was the basis for a return of sinful men to a position of fellowship with God.

But this reconciliation is not limited to men. It applies to the whole order of created being. It is significant that Paul does not here say 'all men', which would be contrary to his normal teaching, but *all things*. The phrase is indefinite and suggests

[1] See Armitage Robinson, *op. cit.*, p. 175.

the completeness of the plan of God. Not only is sinful man reconciled, but the created order which has been made subject to vanity because of sin (see Rom. viii. 20 ff.) will share also in the fruit of the mighty act of atonement on the cross. It is also significant that in this wide sweep of the scope of reconciliation Paul does not include 'things under the earth' as in Philippians ii. 10. There he is dealing with the ultimate sovereignty of Christ; and so he insists that one day even Satan and his hosts will be forced to bend the knee. But here he is dealing with reconciliation and its outcome as seen in a new heaven and a new earth wherein dwells righteousness; but from this all finally rebellious beings, whether devils or men, are excluded.

b. God's purpose for the Colossians (i. 21–23)

21, 22. As always with Paul there is an intensely personal application of these great truths. He has written of God's far-ranging plan of reconciliation; and now he applies it directly to his readers. They may know what is involved in reconciliation when they turn to their own lives, and consider what they were, and what they have become. Formerly, before their experience of the grace of God, they were estranged from God and were, indeed, hostile to Him. This estrangement was not something external, but affected their inmost being. It was their mind with its sinful self-centred attitude which was the source of this rebellion against God and which had left them in the tragic position of being spiritual outcasts. This inner attitude of rebellion had shown itself in wicked deeds, deeds which savoured of the evil one and so were displeasing to God. But by the grace of God the great change has taken place. They have been reconciled.[1] From being aliens and foes

---

[1] It is difficult to decide which reading should be followed. It is possible to follow most of the mss and take it as the aorist 'he reconciled'. This suits the grammar of the verse and accords with the active usage of verse 20. The other possibility is to read, with B, the passive 'you have been reconciled'. This makes the syntax difficult but such a difficulty might attest the genuineness of the reading. If we follow this reading, 'but now . . .' etc. must be taken as a parenthesis.

they have become members of the household of God. But they must always recall that this restoration is rooted in Christ's death. The means of their reconciliation was the Son who took their fleshly nature and as a man died for them. It was no angelic mediator, but the incarnate Son of God, who by means of death effected the return to that status of fellowship with God for which He had created men and from which through sin they had fallen.

The ultimate aim of their reconciliation is that God may present them before Himself in holiness. That the reference here is to the final purpose of God for them, rather than to their present attainments, is seen in the verse which follows and in which continuance is presupposed as a condition of attaining this divinely ordained goal. It is true that the very act of reconciliation carried with it the beginning of the transformation which follows; but the perfecting of that work still lies ahead. They are to be presented to Him in the sense that they will be made fit to stand in His holy presence, and declare eternally the wonder of His grace through what He has accomplished in them. They will be *holy* with a separation from sin and the world, which throughout their life has been a growing experience, and will then be complete. They will be *unblameable*, i.e. spotless, with that purity which is predicated of the Lamb of God, from whom their purity derives. They will be *unreproveable* for, having been justified by the death of Christ, no accusation may be laid against them (also Rom. viii. 33).

23. But such a glorious prospect must not lull them into any spirit of complacency or slackness. God who has ordained the end has also ordained the means, which is their continuing faithfulness. Hence, after his declaration of God's final purpose, Paul adds that he assumes that they will continue in the course in which they have begun. This quality of steady continuance is brought out by the metaphor of the building which stands against every gale. They have been established upon an unshakable foundation, the rock Christ Jesus; and so, being securely *grounded*, they have spiritual stability to enable them to remain steadfast (*settled*) in the face of every blast of temptation or of adversity. Winds of false doctrine too will beat upon them; but they must not be swayed by these. The *hope* of glory which has come to them in the gospel is the strong-point from which they must not be moved. Lest their hold on this sure hope should become weakened, and lest they should feel that their struggle is rather solitary and ineffectual, he reminds them that this gospel has been declared far and wide. They are not an isolated group waging a losing battle for survival. This gospel is God's trumpet call (*kēruchthentos*) to the whole creation, for Paul regards this preaching from the ideal standpoint as being already an accomplished fact. Implicit in the outreach already accomplished is the world-wide preaching which is still in the future. And this gospel which embraces within its purview the whole of creation is the same message which they themselves heard from the lips of Epaphras.

III. PAUL'S PART IN GOD'S PLAN (i. 24—ii. 7)

a. His sufferings (i. 24, 25)

24. The question arises why Paul introduces the personal element here. The answer may be that Paul never ceases to wonder at the privilege that has been given to him of declaring the gospel which he had formerly tried to destroy. Another possibility is that since his apostleship had not, so far as we can see, been questioned in Colossae as elsewhere, here he uses his position to reinforce his call for faithfulness to the apostolic gospel. He is concerned (see ii. 4) lest they should be led astray by the persuasive arguments of false teachers. These men had only to face Epaphras; and the Colossian Christians might feel that, after all, the latter had no greater claim to be authoritative than those who now proposed to be able to lead them further. Hence Paul throws all the weight of his apostolic authority behind the gospel as declared by Epaphras. He stresses that he has been *made* a servant of the gospel. The false teachers are self-appointed

49

guides; but he has behind him the Lord's commission, which enables him to speak with a divinely given authority.

Such a position is no easy one, for it involves suffering. But Paul does not merely accept these *sufferings* as an inevitable accompaniment of his calling. Rather he rejoices in them because they are endured for the sake of the Church. We may see here how far removed is the Christian attitude to suffering from the Stoic. The latter may bear with calm resignation whatever fate may choose to send him. But the Christian goes beyond mere endurance, and rejoices because he sees his sufferings as part of the divine purpose and so he gladly accepts them as a means of fulfilling his part in the eternal plan of God.

Paul emphasizes his reason for rejoicing over his sufferings in words that have probably exercised commentators more than any other passage in this Epistle. Roman Catholic writers have eagerly fastened on the thought of the lack in Christ's sufferings being supplemented by the suffering of the apostle. Here surely is a welcome testimony to their conception of the treasury of merit comprising not only the passion of Christ but also the afflictions of the saints, and dispensed in the form of indulgences. But there are fatal objections to this exegesis of the verse. It would make Paul contradict himself on one of the fundamental issues of his gospel. He is insistent in his writings that Christ's death is a sufficient sacrifice to atone for the sins of His people. To suggest that here he is introducing the thought of imperfection into Christ's atonement is to attribute to him a blatant contradiction of his whole position. Furthermore, he is dealing here at Colossae with a false teaching which denies the sufficiency of the work of Christ, and insists that it must be supplemented by asceticism and other human endeavours. Paul has replied in his opening chapter with an uncompromising stress on the preeminence of Christ, and the completeness of the redemption which He has accomplished. Is it then likely that he would cast this position to the winds and introduce a view which envisaged the perfecting of an incomplete atonement? The very word used here for suffering, *thlipsis*, is nowhere used in the New Testament to describe the atoning death of Christ, and, as Lightfoot points out, it 'certainly would not suggest a sacrificial act'. Finally, it is significant that after speaking of his sufferings for the Church he still calls himself the minister of the Church. But, as Bishop Davenant pointed out, if there were a conception of mediation or expiation in his sufferings he must have referred to himself not as a minister but as a mediator or a redeemer. But if we assume, with Protestant writers, that the idea of expiation is absent here, we are still faced with various possibilities of interpretation. We can dismiss those which interpret the phrase 'the sufferings of Christ' as meaning those demanded by Christ, or those suffered for Christ's sake. The natural meaning of the genitive is to be preferred, unless there are very strong grounds for taking another view; and the only grounds here are a fear lest a wrong idea of expiatory suffering is imported. But as we have seen, such a fear is groundless. If we take the straight-forward meaning of the phrase as signifying Christ's suffering upon earth, we have two main possibilities of interpretation. On the one hand, we may follow Lightfoot and others and refer it to the sufferings involved in the building up of the body of Christ; and in this Christ has left room for further suffering by His servants. On the other hand, we may take these sufferings as being those which Christ suffers in Paul because of the mystical union of the apostle with his Saviour.

This last interpretation has much to commend it. It avoids any suggestion of something lacking in Christ's sufferings. It takes the phrase as a complete whole—'the sufferings of Christ in my flesh'. It fits in well with the conception that Christ suffers in His mystical body so that He could say to Paul on the Damascus Road 'why persecutest thou me?' Thus in Paul's suffering for the Church we can see in a very real sense Christ suffering in a member of His mystical body to build up His Church, just as once He suffered in His physical body to redeem that Church. Those sufferings in Paul's flesh are not yet complete and he is in process of fulfilling them. The compound verb, *antanaplēroō*, suggests the idea of filling up in place of (*anti*) someone else. But it is possible, as C. F. D. Moule points out, to have a verb compounded with one preposition and followed by another. The verb might then recall the phrase just used *for you* (*huper humōn*) and look forward to *for his body's sake* (*huper tou sōmatos autou*). It is for this reason that he rejoices in afflictions because they are within God's plan for the perfecting of His elect. The flesh in which he suffers is of course his own flesh and blood; but lest there should be any misunderstanding he explains that the body of Christ for which he suffers *is the church*.

25. Paul returns to his theme that his relation to the Colossians is by divine appointment. He, in a special sense, (the *I* is emphatic) has been made a servant of the Church. In the household of God he has been given his office (*dispensation*). This appointment has been with a view to their benefit and edification. His task is to develop and fill out with meaning *the word of God*, by declaring to them all that is implicit in the gospel.

b. The mystery of Christ (i. 26–28)

26. This gospel message has lain as a hidden thing from eternity; but has now been openly declared. Lightfoot suggests that the term *mystery* has been borrowed by Paul from the mystery cults, each of which had their secrets to which their initiates were introduced. The Pauline conception of a secret once hidden, but now revealed, would then be a Christian adaptation of a conception in current use, but standing in marked contrast to the esoteric usage of the mystery cults. But we are equally justified in looking for an Old Testament background, in view of the fact that the word is used in the Gospels (Mt. xiii. 11; Lk. viii. 10), where there can hardly be any polemic reference. In Daniel ii. 19, 28, 29 (LXX), the term is used to describe a secret which is hidden in the counsels of God and is revealed only to His servants. This surely was behind Christ's language concerning the mysteries of the kingdom. For Paul, then, the mystery *par excellence* is the secret, long veiled in the purposes of God, and now revealed to His apostles, and through them to the faithful, that the Gentiles are also heirs of the promise of the indwelling Christ.

This open secret was formerly hidden *from ages and from generations*. It has been suggested, e.g. by E. F. Scott,[1] that these refer to angelic powers such as are described by these titles in the gnostic hierarchy; and in view of the similar passage in Ephesians iii. 5–10, where Paul speaks not only of men but also of angels as those from whom the secret was withheld, this is a possible position. A similar view appears in Bengel's[2] suggestion that *ages* refers to angels and *generations* to men. The context here in Colossians however speaks of men as being the objects of the revelation. It is possible therefore to take *ages and generations* in their literal sense. The thought then would be that through all the ages of time and from all the generations of men this secret was hidden, but it has now been revealed to God's people.

27. It is God's eternal purpose (*ēthelēsen*) that His people should know the wonder of this mystery. Paul is so exultant that he piles up words to describe the marvel of God's disclosure. *Glory* is used of the effulgence to men of the divine character. So this disclosure of the mystery shines forth with a light which declares the inner wonder of the eternal purpose of God. But he intensifies the thought by speaking of *the riches* of this glory. God's purpose has flamed forth in a blaze of light among the Gentiles who formerly walked in darkness.

The very heart of the mystery is the indwelling of Christ *among the Gentiles*, as a pledge of final glory. (*You* in this context obviously refers to the Gentiles.) Already the light has shone. Yet this is but the dawn of the new day which will reach its zenith at the second coming. That the Messiah should come among His people was a thought which no Jew would find

[1] *Colossians, Philemon and Ephesians* (*Moffatt New Testament Commentaries*), 1948.
[2] *Gnomon of the New Testament*, Vol. IV, 1873.

strange. But that the Messiah of Israel should dwell among the Gentiles was an entirely new revelation of the purposes of God.

28. This Christ, who has been declared to be central in the purpose of God, is also central in the apostolic proclamation. The word *we* is emphatic and stresses the difference between Paul, Timothy and Epaphras, and the false teachers at Colossae. The latter spoke of other mediators and esoteric practices which were superficially attractive; but for the apostolic group Christ is pre-eminent, and He is the very heart of their message. Their preaching is neither easy in its demands, nor shallow in its content. The emphasis on repentance is brought out by the note of warning. The depth of the message is stressed in the mention of teaching. We may recall Paul's description of his preaching to the Ephesian elders as being summed up in the words 'repentance toward God, and faith toward our Lord Jesus Christ' (Acts xx. 21). The source of the preaching is not human knowledge; nor is it a restricted set of religious theories, but the whole sweep of the *wisdom* which is from above. This wisdom, which is the practical application of a divinely given knowledge, is, as it were, the sphere in which the apostolic instructor moves. The aim of the teaching is that each one who responds may be presented spiritually mature before God. It is not necessary to follow Lightfoot's suggestion that Paul borrows the word *perfect, teleios*, from the mystery cults, in view of the usage of the word elsewhere in the New Testament to connote maturity (e.g. Mt. v. 48, xix. 21, etc.). The background of the preaching is the universal aspect of the gospel. This is brought out by the repetition of the word *all*, and indirectly reflects on the false exclusiveness of those who would restrict the path to spiritual maturity to those who adopted their tenets.

c. Paul's prayer for his readers (i. 29—ii. 5)

29. Paul has spoken of his aim in preaching, but he must add from his own experience that such an aim is not easily achieved by the preacher of the gospel. He draws his metaphor from the athlete, both in training and in the contest. Such preaching involves steady toil, and an intense concentration of every fibre of the preacher's being. Yet, as always, there is a complementary truth. Amid the spiritual conflict he experiences the inner working of the Spirit of Christ. This activity within is accompanied by a power which far surpasses mere human endeavour. We do not need to take *mightily* here in a restricted sense as a reference to the ability to work miracles; but it certainly does point to a special enabling which is the result of the activity of God.

ii. 1. Paul's general concern for the churches is seen further in his particular care for the Christians of the Lycus valley. (Since Laodicea is mentioned here and in iv. 15, 16 it is likely that the church there was also infected with the same false teaching as Colossae. But the fact that Colossae is the primary goal of the letter suggests that the danger was more acute there.) Here we see the warm pastoral spirit with which the apostle of the Gentiles was so richly endued. The one who had urged the Ephesian elders to 'feed the church of God' was himself possessed of a pastoral care which was both deep and broad. The depth is reflected in the intense travail of soul involved in his praying for them. The arena, which was the scene of desperate struggles for mastery, was an apt metaphor to describe the inner conflict of one who was engaged in earnest intercession for them. The width of his pastoral care is demonstrated by the fact that he is not only concerned with those with whom he has had personal contact. His loving desire that the people of God should be built up reaches far beyond the churches God has used him directly to bring into being, to those who had not seen him in the flesh, but with whom he still felt a close spiritual affinity, and for whom he maintained a sense of pastoral responsibility.

2. The burden of Paul's prayer is first that their hearts may be strengthened. In view of the debilitating effect of false

teaching upon the spiritual life and of the confusion brought
to the church by the cross-winds of diverse doctrines, this
inner strengthening was a primary need. He prays further
that they may be *knit together* into a unity in which the uniting
principle is *love*. This petition for their unity looks both to
what has preceded in his prayer, and to what follows. He has
prayed for strengthening; and one of the great means which
God uses for such a purpose is the fellowship of His people.
Error is divisive. It breaks up the unity of the body of believers.
Thus the unifying power of a God-given love for Christ and for
one another will be a means of resisting this spiritual corrosion
from without. But the prayer also looks to what follows. Paul
goes on to pray for their growth in spiritual understanding.
But it is characteristic of him to think of such a growth as being
no mere individual experience but rather in the context of
fellowship, just as in Ephesians iii. 18 he prays that they may
be able to comprehend 'with all saints'. So here he desires
that as a united body they may be led into all the wealth that
comes when the *understanding*[1] reaches a settled conviction.
Plērophoria, translated in the AV *full assurance*, bears throughout
its usage in the New Testament the same meaning of a sure
conviction to which a man is led. Thus here it stands in sharp
contrast with the trembling indecision of mere religious
speculation which leads to spiritual impoverishment. When
the understanding is controlled by the Spirit of God, it is led
to a full assurance concerning the truths of God, and this is
indeed an abundantly rich experience. The ultimate goal of
his prayer is that they may attain a deep knowledge[2] of the
mystery of God. Since the mystery now lies open, it is no
longer a contradiction to speak of knowing the mystery. The
unveiled secret is simply Christ Himself.

There is a rather bewildering array of variant readings here
but the most likely one is *tou theou Christou*. Not only is this the
reading of B with a strong attestation from Hilary; but, as
Lightfoot points out in a note on the readings, it can be shown
to underlie the other variations. It is true that some would

[1] On *sunesis* see i. 9.　　　　[2] On *epignōsis* see i. 6.

56

contend for the even shorter reading *tou theou*; but the MS evidence for this is not sufficiently early. If we accept the reading of B, it is possible to interpret it in one of three ways—either taking *Christ* in apposition to *God*, or dependent upon *God*, or in apposition to *mystery*. Apart from arguments drawn from Paul's usage elsewhere, the context here would seem to be a major consideration. Paul has just spoken in i. 27 of Christ as being Himself the mystery and the *for* of ii. 1 links his prayer closely to what has preceded; this strongly suggests that the correct interpretation is that which takes *Christ* in apposition to *mystery*.

3. In Christ *the treasures of wisdom and knowledge* are hidden, not in the sense of being utterly beyond our reach, but rather as treasures in a mine which has already been opened, and from which by diligent search a constant supply of precious stones may be extracted. Wisdom and knowledge are linked together also in Romans xi. 33 and 1 Corinthians xii. 8. In each case the same order is observed, which suggests that wisdom is the comprehensive view of the truth of God given by the Spirit of God, while knowledge is the apprehension of particular truths. The former refers to spiritual insight, the latter to the grasp of specific truths of the gospel. For the Christian these two are linked together because it is due to a divinely given wisdom that he can reach a higher knowledge than would come by purely natural reasoning. At Colossae the false teachers no doubt spoke much about the knowledge they professed to teach. But for Paul the only true knowledge must spring from wisdom, and together they have their source in Christ. He does not merely give some truths which may be supplemented by those given by another religious teacher, for *all* the treasures, the sum total of the wealth, of wisdom and knowledge are found in Him.

4. The apostle has not however drawn aside the veil from his soul for any purpose of self-glorification; but in order to give his readers the strength of his sympathy, and by his concern for them, to stimulate them to hold firmly to the truth of the gospel. Thus he emphasizes the fact that he speaks thus to guard them against false teaching. He has spoken of Christ as being the only real source of wisdom and knowledge in order to show the utter contrast between the truth of God and the erroneous speculations of the false teachers. Their theories mislead because they spring from faulty reasoning, the fallacy of which is clouded by the persuasive arguments with which they are advocated. Such *enticing words* may have a specious appearance of being true; but if the believer will but pause and reflect he will see that they are very different from the powerful demonstration which the Spirit gives.[1]

5. Paul continues with a further explanation of his personal emphasis—hence the introductory *for* at the beginning of the verse. Just as he once wrote to the Corinthians, so here he maintains that bodily absence does not mean a complete separation, for in spirit he is with them. This sense of a fellowship which distance cannot sever, coupled with the spirit of thanksgiving on their behalf disclosed in his earlier prayer, leads to a deep joy. This rejoicing in turn leads him to contemplate (*beholding* speaks of more than a merely cursory glance) their orderly fellowship and their strong faith. *Taxin* means an ordered arrangement. Lightfoot sees in it a military metaphor, but as Abbott points out, it only takes this military colouring from its context, and might as readily refer to the ordering of the state or the household. If we look at the New Testament usage, it upholds Abbott's contention, for *taxis* is applied to the order of the priesthood.[2] The order which is here a cause for joy recalls Paul's earlier thanksgiving for the Colossians' love for the saints. In spite of the divisive tendency of wrong teaching he sees a compact fellowship, and this order rejoices his heart. *Stereōma, the stedfastness*, is rendered by the Vulgate *firmamentum*; which looks back to the LXX version of Genesis i. 6

---

[1] For the contrast between *enticing words* and the Spirit's demonstration, cf. 1 Cor. ii. 4.
[2] Lk. i. 8; Heb. v. 6 etc.

where *stereōma* is also used. The essential element in the word is that of strength. Thus Luke uses the equivalent verb to describe the strengthening of the ankle bones of the paralytic.[1] Paul, then, is rejoicing in the stability of their faith. But he adds a further note. It is a Christ-centred faith. Earlier he had spoken of their faith 'in Christ' and used the preposition *en*, making Christ its source. Here he uses *eis* which views faith from the point of view of its object. But whether it be as the source of faith or as the object of faith, Christ is at the very heart of their spiritual experience: He is the beginning and the end, the alpha and omega of their faith. The pre-eminence of Christ is the prime theme of the Epistle. How Paul therefore rejoices that these Colossian believers are demonstrating this pre-eminence not merely in word but in life.

d. A call to continuance (ii. 6, 7)

6. The *therefore* looks back to the apostle's previous statement about their stable faith. This initial acceptance of the gospel is to be the pattern of their continuing faithfulness. To receive, *paralambano*, may be used, not only in its literal sense of taking someone along with oneself, but also (as in 1 Corinthians xv.1) of receiving from others a tradition. Thus the Colossians had received the apostolic gospel centring on the Person of Christ. The aorist tense suggests the decisive character of their reception of the Word. Faith had laid hold, not merely on a human tradition, but on a Person. It was the Christ, the only begotten Son of God, whom they had received. The order of the title here underscores the constant emphasis of the Epistle on the divine nature of the Son. He is first *Christ;* but faith saw in Him *Jesus* the Saviour, the One who stooped to man's need by Himself becoming man, and bearing the guilt of man's sins. And faith, in obedience, had acknowledged that this Saviour must be Lord. This title, which recalls the personal name Jehovah in the Old Testament, had been to them the declaration of His absolute demands upon them, and to that declaration faith had said its deep 'Amen'.

[1] Acts iii. 7.

Thus it was Christ in all His fullness who had been the object of their initial act of faith. It is Christ also who must be the very sphere of their spiritual growth and development. They are to *walk* in dependence upon Him. Walking speaks of the normal pattern of living. It suggests the steady progress of the one who is patiently going on in face of temptation to turn aside, or to be discouraged. But Paul, as often, is not confined to one metaphor. He moves quickly to the pictures of the growing plant, and the growing building, to give a full illustration of the developing Christian life.

7. The tenses here are significant. *Rooted* is the perfect participle. This suggests the thought of something which took place in the past, but whose effects persist in the present. The 'rooting by faith' meant an organic union with Christ, so that now there is a perennial source of life for the growth of the spiritual plant. *Built up* is the present participle, and speaks of the steady growth of the structure. Paul does not use the preposition *epi* which would direct the thought towards the foundation. That aspect has been covered in the metaphor of the rooted plant. Here the preposition *en* suggests rather the fact that Christ is the means whereby the fabric is held together. Thus there is a common feature in both metaphors. Christ is the life of the plant and He is the binding force of the building.

The third participle stems from the two previous ones. It speaks of the continuous strengthening (again the present participle) which follows from this Christ-centred living. It is possible to take the phrase *in the faith* in different ways. Lightfoot makes it a dative of instrument and renders it 'by your faith'. But it would seem better to take faith in the objective sense as the body of revealed truth, in view of the following reference to being taught, and in view of the whole context of the passage with its warning against false teaching.

But they are not merely to hold to the faith which they were taught. They are to increase in their knowledge of it, and in their experience of its power in their lives. The verb *perisseuō* moves from the sense of having abundance, to that of excelling. Thus Paul desires that they might be outstanding in their grasp and application of the faith. But lest such spiritual excellence should bring the snare of self-praise in its train he introduces a typically Pauline note of thanksgiving. Negatively this lifts a man's thoughts from himself, for true thanksgiving is begotten in humility. Positively it directs a man's heart towards God, from whom all his growth is derived, and to whom, therefore, praise and glory should alone be given.

IV. WARNING AGAINST FALSE TEACHING (ii. 8-23)

a. Philosophy and truth (ii. 8, 9)

8. The warning is introduced by a call to vigilance. The present tense suggests a constant watchfulness on their part, lest they should be led astray. The AV translation *spoil* gives the literal meaning of *sulagōgeō* which is to lead into captivity. Paul had spoken earlier of the mighty deliverance which had come to them through the gospel (i. 12, 13). To revert then to a man-made religious system after knowing the liberating power of Christ would be nothing else but a return to bondage. The way in which the warning is couched—*sulagōgōn* is a present participle—suggests that Paul is not warning against a hypothetical possibility but against an actually impending danger.

The word *philosophy* here is obviously linked closely with the phrase *vain deceit*, for the definite article precedes only the former word. Hence the phrase is descriptive of the philosophy. It is empty for it is void of real truth. It is empty of vital power, for the dynamic of the gospel is absent. It is empty of hope, for it leads away from the light of God's presence into the mists of man's speculation. It is deceitful because of its attractive presentation which seduces the minds of those who are drawn away by it, and which conceals its own utter barrenness. The question arises as to whether Paul completely condemns philosophy itself or only a perversion of it. In the early Church there were those who would say that philosophy was no enemy of the gospel; and might indeed, like Judaism, be a preparation for it. There were others who saw philosophy as productive only of error. With Paul it would no doubt be true to say that philosophy, in the simple sense of a love of knowledge and a desire for the truth, would be quite compatible with his position. But to philosophy in the developed sense with its emphasis on the primacy of human reason he would obviously be utterly opposed. For Paul, the gospel was rooted in revelation. God had spoken clearly and finally in Christ. The believer comes in humility to hear what God has to say to him. His reason is applied to understand the wisdom which is revealed in Christ. Thus, Pauline theology is God-centred in contrast to any humanistic philosophy which begins with man, and which makes man's reason the measure of truth. The introductory chapters of 1 Corinthians show this contrast between the wisdom of the world and the wisdom of God. Hence, while the Christian may see a certain negative value in speculative philosophy, he will constantly be on his guard lest he come to study revelation, not as a believer, but as a humanist. This does not mean that he should come with a blind unreasoning faith. But it does mean that, instead of bringing philosophical presuppositions which will colour his study of Scripture and so prejudice his interpretation, he comes as one conscious of the finiteness of his intellect, and aware that his mind also is affected by his sinful nature. Thus he is willing to be taught by the Holy Spirit, and acknowledges that it is the Word of God rather than his own reason which is the final arbiter of truth.

This philosophy is described further by three phrases which show the pattern of this development. It is drawn from *the tradition of men* rather than from the revelation of God. It is inspired by *the rudiments of the world*. This latter phrase has occasioned much discussion, and we must not be over-dogmatic as to its precise meaning. The word *stoicheia* means literally the elements of learning or the physical elements of the natural world. Hence it could mean here rudimentary principles of instruction fitted for childhood, but not for man-

hood. The thought would then be that to return to philoso-
phic speculation would be to cast away the mature teaching
of the gospel for the poverty-stricken opinions of an immature
religion which draws its being not from God but from this
world. This interpretation is possible, but it does not seem as
adequate to meet the implications of the context of the passage
as does the interpretation which takes *rudiments* as referring to
the unseen hosts of evil which were, in the false teaching,
linked with the physical elements. This is the view underlying
the RSV translation 'the elemental spirits of the universe'.
We do not need to narrow this view down, as some have done,
to apply it only to the heavenly bodies which had become an
object of worship. This might be so if the only manifestation
of the error was in terms of observance of festivals, new moons,
etc. But it will be seen that such observance was only part of
the false teaching. The more general application to the spiritual forces of this world does justice to the contrast which
follows. Over against the bankruptcy of these spiritual powers
is set the majesty of Christ as reflected in His divine fullness,
His headship over every power, and His mighty victory over
them at Calvary. A confirmation of this interpretation may be
found in Galatians iv, where Paul speaks again about the
stoicheia, which in verses 8 and 9 seem to be clearly linked with
the beings that 'by nature are no gods'. The final indictment
of the false doctrine is that it does not accord with the truth
as it is revealed in Christ.

9. If in Christ the fullness of the Godhead dwells, then He is
the source of all truth, and any teaching which does not accord
with Him is at once declared to be false. This statement of
Christ's essential deity is fuller than the earlier one in i. 19.
Trench[1] points out the important difference between *theotēs*
used here and translated by the AV *Godhead* and *theiotēs* which
is similarly translated in Romans i. 20. *Theiotēs* speaks of
divinity as reflected in various ways. Thus, in Romans Paul
is saying that the glory of nature declares the majesty and

[1] *Synonyms of the New Testament,* 1876, p. 6.

power of God. Yet he would not say that nature reveals God as a person as He is revealed in Christ. But here he does not wish to state merely that divine qualities are revealed in Christ. He is rather insisting that in Christ dwells the very essence of God, and so he uses the word *theotēs* to convey this idea of essential Godhead.

This indwelling of the fullness of God is firmly linked with the incarnate Christ. It has been suggested, in view of the contrast in verse 17 between *skia* ('shadow') and *sōma* ('substance'), that *sōmatikōs* should be taken here in the sense of 'really' or 'essentially'. Thus God dwelt in the prophets in the Old Testament, but not in the abiding and essential way in which He indwells the Son. A similar view is seen in Augustine who contrasted the dwelling in types and figures in the temple with the substantial dwelling in Christ. But the context does not call for such contrasts, and indeed both Abbott and Lightfoot insist that any other meaning than *bodily* cannot be supported by the usage of the word. It is surely more in accord with Paul's reaction to false teaching to find him asserting that in the incarnate One we see the very nature of God. This accords too with John's teaching concerning the *Logos* (Jn. i. 1, 14) who was essentially God, but who became flesh. It is however the incarnate Christ in His glorified state of whom Paul speaks, for the indwelling is a fact of the present time (*katoikei*). The One who at Bethlehem took human nature, now in heaven still retains His glorified humanity and in Him the very essence of deity has its eternal dwelling-place.

b. New men in Christ (ii. 10–15)

10. But if in Christ the fullness of Godhead dwells, then this has profound consequences for His people. They are *in him* by a spiritual union, which means that they share His life. Hence they share His *plērōma*; and so are partakers of the very nature of God. This is echoed in John's similar assertion that the Word is full of grace and truth, from which he concludes that 'of his fulness have all we received'. Here Paul counters any suggestion from the false teaching that by ritual observances a man may hope one day to attain to a share in the *plērōma*. In Christ that experience is already a fact. They have already been made partakers of the divine nature (hence the perfect participle *peplērōmenoi*). Further they do not need to depend on angelic mediators to attain some future spiritual goal, for the Christ who has already imparted to them the life of God, is Himself the sovereign head of every angelic being.[1]

While we can see that the direct reference of the verb, *plēroō*, is to the noun *plērōma*, and speaks of the sharing in the divine fullness, it has also, by virtue of this work of grace, a reference to the purpose for which man was created. The fall of man has led to a condition of incompleteness. Unregenerate man is spiritually incomplete, for he is out of touch with God. He is morally incomplete, for he lacks both the final standard of conduct which is the will of God, and the dynamic which is the indwelling of God's Spirit. He is mentally incomplete, for sin has vitiated even his reasoning power; and he cannot understand spiritual truths. Hence it is only through the miracle of regeneration in which, through union with Christ, he partakes of the life of God, that he reaches his completeness. It is only then that his human nature is filled out with meaning. He is spiritually complete for he is now reconciled to God, and in fellowship with his Creator. He is morally complete, not in the sense of being perfect, but in that he now recognizes the final authority of the will of God, and already experiences the energizing of God's Spirit, which is a foretaste of that perfection which will accompany his glorification. He is mentally complete, not in the sense of having all knowledge, but inasmuch as his mind is now enlightened by the Spirit of God to discern spiritual truths to which, formerly, he was blind.

11. Gentile Christians have no need of the rite of circumcision, for they have received from Christ the spiritual circumci-

---

[1] The reading *hōs* is to be preferred to *hō*, although the latter is in B. It would be contrary to normal usage to speak of the fullness, rather than Christ, being the *head*. Further the *en hō* of verse 11 would also have to be referred to the *plērōma* and this is ruled out by the context.

sion of which that rite was a type. The bodily circumcision of the Old Testament was the divinely given seal of membership of the covenant people. It spoke of the removal of sin, and by its association with the process of generation stressed the sin inherent in our fallen nature as the offspring of Adam. Hence positively it was the sign of acceptance with God, as Paul clearly states in Romans iv. 11, when speaking of Abraham. But even in the Old Testament there is the constant emphasis on the fact that circumcision is not merely something outward. While, admittedly, it is given by God, and testifies to the gracious acceptance of sinful men, yet it does also call for obedience. Thus true circumcision is not just a matter of the flesh, but of the heart, and a man may wear the outward badge and yet be treated as the uncircumcised Gentiles (Je. iv. 4, ix. 25). This Old Testament insistence on the inwardness of circumcision finds its fulfilment in Christ. His circumcision is essentially a spiritual act—it is *made without hands*, and it brings to the believer the blessings of which circumcision in the flesh spoke. In Christ the believer has been made a member of the new Israel, the covenant people. In Christ he has been accepted by God.

But there was a further significance in the rite of circumcision which finds its fulfilment here. The actual form of the rite, dealing as it did with the organ of procreation, emphasized that it was human nature as such that was unclean and needed cleansing. It is not the act of procreation which is sinful, but the product of that act, namely human nature. Thus circumcision spoke vividly of the cutting away of what was unclean, that the man might be acceptable to God. It spoke not only of justification, in that it referred to his status, but it spoke also of regeneration, in that it declared that a radical change must take place in his nature. So Paul is here insisting that the man who is in Christ has broken with his past. He has put off the body of the flesh. The flesh is human nature in its fallen condition. And by the body of the flesh he means human nature as an organized whole. It is the sum total of all that is evil in the old man. Now in the spiritual renewal which has come through union with Christ, the believer has repudiated his old nature. This does not mean that it has ceased to exist, for Paul will presently urge that it must be mortified. It does mean that the believer must adopt a new attitude to it. Formerly when he was 'in Adam' he was dominated by his fallen nature; but now he is 'in Christ' and that sinful nature has been 'put off'. He must realize that he is a new man and as such must assert his new authority over the sin which still dwells in his members but which is now an alien power and will one day be finally and eternally destroyed.

12. This putting away of the old nature was openly declared in Christian baptism, which is the visible covenant-seal of the new Israel, just as circumcision was of the old. The picture of being buried beneath the water and rising again is a vivid portrayal of the same truth as that which circumcision has been declaring; for the old man is buried that the new man may rise. The question arises as to whether it is correct to follow the AV *wherein* which refers to the preceding word baptism, or whether we should translate *in whom* as referring to Christ. In favour of the latter is the parallelism with the opening words of verse 11 *in whom also*. But in favour of the AV is the more telling parallelism between *buried with him* and *risen*. The fact that the latter is also a compound verb with the prefix *sun* almost demands that the parallel be enforced: buried with Him— risen with Him. But this radical transformation is not due to any human power or insight. It is effected through faith in the God who has declared His power in raising Christ from the dead. Some have taken *energeias* as a subjective genitive, and interpreted it as being the source of faith. It is however more in accord with normal usage in the New Testament to take it as an objective genitive.[1] The mighty working of God as already demonstrated in the resurrection of Christ is thus the object of the believer's confidence. The argument would then be as follows: they had accepted the fact of Christ's resurrection. This was the signal demonstration of the power of God,

[1] See e.g. Mk. xi. 22; Rom. iii. 22, 26; Gal. ii. 16, 20, iii. 22.

and in reliance upon that power they had known a spiritual resurrection in union with Christ.

13. At first sight it might seem as if this were merely a repetition of the previous verse. But the very strong emphasis on the words *and you* shows that Paul is now applying his general statement to believers more specifically to the Colossians. What is here brought into prominence is their former condition as Gentiles, from which they have been delivered. Formerly they were spiritually dead. This deadness was reflected both in their actual trespasses and in the sinful nature from which those transgressions sprang. We take *en* here to mean, not that the trespasses and sinful nature were the *cause* of death, but rather the *sphere* in which the deadness was manifested. *Paraptōma* speaks of a falling away from the pathway of obedience to God, and so is an apt word to describe the life of active sinfulness which means turning aside from the will of God. As to the phrase *the uncircumcision of your flesh*, the parallel passage in Ephesians ii helps to reveal the meaning. These Gentiles were literally uncircumcised, in contrast to the Jews who had the circumcision in the flesh. This uncircumcised state however spoke also of their hopeless spiritual condition outside the people of God, which made them strangers to the covenant with its rich promise of forgiveness and reconciliation to God. But the context here in Colossians brings out the meaning even further. Paul has been speaking of the circumcision of Christ as involving a repudiation of the old nature. Thus the literal uncircumcision of these Gentiles was but a symbol of the fact that they were subject to their old sinful nature until God in mercy had raised them from spiritual death, and, through their union with Christ, had made them spiritually alive. But this great act of spiritual renewal involves also the forgiveness of sins. The forgiveness springs from the free unmerited favour of God—the verb *charizomai* has the obvious link with *charis* and stresses that pardon is due to the grace of God. It covers not only past sins but all sins, for the atonement is the mighty act of reconciliation which has laid, once and for all, an abiding basis for continued pardon for the people of God.

14. The question arises here as to the subject of the verbs— is it still *God*, or is Lightfoot right in saying that we must suppose a change to *Christ* either before the participle *blotting out* or before the verb *took out of the way*? But to postulate such a change of subject is to make an arbitrary interference with the grammar of the passage in which the subject clearly is the same throughout. Thus it is quite clear that 'God' is the subject in verse 13 as being the One who raised us with Christ. But the participle of verse 13 is paralleled by that of verse 14 which would naturally have the same subject. Further the *and* before *took*, *ērken*, links it with the previous verse and leads to the conclusion that the subject of both is the same. The difficulty largely goes if we recall that it is quite in accord with Paul's normal mode of thinking for him to speak of the cross in terms of the activity of God. Thus if we take *en autō* in verse 15 as meaning 'in Him', we have the thought that all that was accomplished on the cross was the work of God in Christ.

This divinely planned work of atonement meant for us a cancellation of debt. A *cheirographon* (*handwriting*) was a statement of debt signed by the debtor in token of his acknowledgement of his indebtedness. Thus the law of God with its specific ordinances stands as God's statement of our indebtedness; and when once we are awakened by the Spirit, our conscience acknowledges that the claims of divine justice are absolutely righteous, and that we are hopelessly in debt. The Greek Fathers took *tois dogmasin*, *ordinances*, as referring to the ordinances of the gospel; but this fails to notice the parallel between these and the verb *dogmatizesthe* ('are ye subject to ordinances', in verse 20) which obviously speaks of legal ordinances. This bond was not only against us in the sense of stating the claims against us, but was also *contrary to us* inasmuch as it stood as our foe. The law of God not only stated our guilt, but cried out for the penalty due to such guilt. So the bond was our enemy.

Hence the wonder of the atonement is that God has wiped away, as one erases writing from a book, the awful indictment which stood against us. But added to the picture of the erasure of the writing on the bond is that of the bond itself being removed. To speak of removing something 'out of the midst' is an idiomatic way of describing the removal of an obstacle. Hence the cancelling of the bond meant the removal of that which hindered fellowship with God. The perfect tense of the verb then brings out more fully the thought that what was done on the cross has a present abiding significance. The cancellation of the bond was effected by Christ's death. Thus it is pictured as being nailed once and for all (the aorist tense stands in contrast to the preceding perfect) to the cross. Hence the cross which meant the death of Christ meant also the death of the law which ceased to have its power over the people of God. Because Christ not only perfectly fulfilled the law, but also stood in the sinner's place and accepted in His own Person the penalty due to the one who breaks the law, the very bond itself has been cancelled. Wordsworth fails to penetrate to the heart of Paul's thinking when he imagines that because the moral law is of abiding significance Paul must be speaking only of ceremonial law. Paul clearly distinguishes law as a means of justification, in which role it is primarily negative in purpose in that it only shows a man his guilt and his help-lessness, and thus leads him through self-despair to faith in Christ; and law as a statement of the holy demands of God, to which the believer once justified will yield evangelical obedi-ence. It is the law viewed as the instrument of condemnation that has been dealt with. It no longer binds, for in Christ God has liberated His people from the penalty which it demanded Because the law has been satisfied completely, it has ceased to have any power to condemn and in this sense has been removed as far as they are concerned.

15. But the cross meant not only the cancellation of the bond but also the conquest of the powers of evil. The victory is pictured here in terms of the triumphant Roman General who strips his foes and leads them as captives behind his chariot in his victory procession. The word *spoiled* has occasioned much discussion. For Lightfoot it is really the crucial reason for his insistence that we must postulate a change of subject. He insists that the verb, being in the middle voice, requires that we translate 'stripped from himself'. This he says could only refer to Christ and not to the Father, and he pictures Christ as throwing aside like soiled clothing the powers of evil which clung to Him. But surely we cannot speak of Christ having the powers of evil in such an intimate connection with His humanity. We have 'put off the old man' (iii. 9), but for Christ the powers of evil were always external, and never succeeded in establishing themselves in His perfect humanity as they have done in our fallen nature. Furthermore, the picture of stripping off clothing does not accord with the other verbs with their metaphor of the triumphant procession. Abbott suggests that the middle should be taken simply as expressing a personal interest; and H. C. G. Moule agrees with this, with his suggestion 'stripping them (i.e. of their possessions) for Himself'. Hence the apparently active sense of the AV is quite a legitimate rendering. God, in Christ, stripped from the powers of evil their hold over the lives of men. Some, of course, have questioned whether the evil powers are here intended; and Abbott, rather tentatively, follows the suggestion that it is the angelic powers who were the mediators of the law. But surely such angelic powers as were used in the giving of the law were the servants of God. But the powers here pictured are essentially foes who have been brought into subjection. To Abbott's question as to what the disarming of the hostile powers had to do with the abolition of the *dogmata*, the answer would seem to be in the following paragraph. Paul there calls for a rejection both of legalism and also of submission to angelic beings. But this twofold call is based on the statement of verses 14 and 15 that the cross has meant the death of the law, and the defeat of the hosts of evil.

The evil powers thus despoiled were openly exhibited in their hour of defeat. Since *deigmatizō* itself speaks of making a

71

public spectacle of someone, the phrase *en parrēsia* would be rather repetitive if we merely translated it *openly*. If, however, we give it its normal Pauline meaning of 'boldly', or 'with confidence', it adds to the picture of the conqueror who exhibits his vanquished foes with the sure confidence of one whose triumph is complete, and who leads a procession of utterly defeated captives. It is difficult to be certain about the meaning of the phrase *en autō* (*in it*). Many commentators refer it to the cross which is here viewed as the chariot of the conqueror. This would be a possible interpretation if Christ were the subject of the sentence. But if, as we have maintained, God is the subject, then the phrase more naturally refers to Christ, just as in the only other context where Paul uses the verb *thriambeuō* (2 Cor. ii. 14) the parallel phrase *en tō Christō* is used. In any case, the two interpretations converge, for it is, after all, in Christ crucified that God has effected His final victory.

c. Christian liberty (ii. 16-23)

16. Since Christ has abrogated the law by His death the Colossians must therefore resist any attempt to ensnare them in a new bondage to legalistic requirements. Whether in the matter of ceremonially eating or drinking unclean foods or drinks, or in the matter of the observance of special days such as the annual, monthly, or weekly festivals, they must resist any pressure to make them conform to legal demands, for the law as an instrument of condemnation has been nailed to the cross. No man can judge them, for the very basis on which he would bring his unfavourable verdict, namely the law, has been cancelled. Here, as in the Epistle to the Galatians, is Paul's insistence on the liberty of the Christian man who has been delivered by Christ from bondage to a set of rules.

17. The Christian lives in the era of fulfilment. Hence the ordinances of the law must be viewed, not as abiding realities which are therefore still binding, but rather as types which have found their fulfilment in Christ. *A shadow* has no permanent reality apart from *the body* which projects it. Indeed when the body stands directly beneath the light the shadow disappears. Thus the law only had significance in relationship to Christ to whom it pointed. Christ indeed stands in the full blaze of revelation, and the shadow which in earlier stages pointed to His coming has now gone, and in its place is the reality of the gospel.

18. The AV margin probably gives a better rendering of the verb *katabrabeuō* which here makes its only appearance in biblical Greek. The meaning in classical Greek varies from the more specific 'to deprive of a prize' to the more general 'to give an adverse judgment'. In view of Paul's fondness for metaphors drawn from the stadium (witness his picture in Philippians iii. 14 of the athlete striving to win the prize, *brabeion*) it would be most appropriate here to see the heretical teachers assuming to themselves the position of arbiters and disqualifying the Colossian believers for failing to keep their ritualistic rules. Thus it would be a more vivid repetition of the 'let no man . . . judge you' of verse 16.

It is extremely difficult to decide how the participle *thelōn* should be taken, and commentators have varied. C. F. D. Moule, following Lightfoot, suggests that it is 'a barbarism derived from the Semitic idiom of the LXX', and interprets it in the sense 'delighting in'. Abbott however maintains that Paul does not thus violate Greek grammar. He would connect *thelōn* with the participle *embateuōn* and follow the RV margin 'of his own mere will, by humility, etc.'. In favour of the first interpretation is the fact that there are a group of four participles in this verse, and it would seem natural to take them all in a similar fashion rather than isolating the first one and taking it adverbially. In addition, the interpretation 'delighting in' fits the context and gives a more likely meaning than any such rendering as 'gladly' or 'willingly'. A further confirmation is found in the compound *ethelothrēskeia* ('will worship'), in verse 23, which strongly suggests that in verse 18 *thelōn* and *thrēskeia* should be taken together.

Normally humility is considered a virtue by Paul, but here

he is obviously dealing with a false type of humility. On the one side it is qualified by the phrase 'delighting in'; but a humility in which one delights is obviously no humility at all. On the other hand, it is linked with worship of angels, and this puts it in the category of disobedience, for in their apparent humility before angelic mediators these heretical teachers are really refusing to acknowledge the one Mediator before whom alone they should bow in reverence.

The phrase that follows is so difficult, not only as to the correct reading, but also as to the interpretation, that some have been driven to suspect corruption of the text. But any emendations are purely conjectural, and rather than embark on such textual speculation it seems best to confine ourselves to a consideration of the two main MS traditions. The difficulty then is that the two readings are completely opposed, for one has a negative (either *mē* or *ouk*) while the other has not. The Received Text with the negative is suspect on two counts. On the one hand the weight of MS evidence favours the omission of the negative. On the other hand the fact that the insertion of the negative solves the problem of rendering the difficult word *embateuōn, intruding,* leads us to see how the negative could have been introduced. But in assessing the evidence it is usually better to prefer the more difficult reading especially when that reading has the additional weight of MS evidence behind it. Thus while the AV does justice to the word *embateuōn* we cannot feel justified in doing as H. C. G. Moule does and accepting the Received Text.

Assuming then that there is no negative, we face the extremely difficult question as to how to render *embateuōn*, since this is the only occurrence of the word in the New Testament, and from its usage elsewhere it is difficult to find a meaning which suits this context. The RV mg. gives an attractive rendering 'taking his stand' which certainly fits in with the context; but there is no evidence from the usage of the word elsewhere to justify this rendering. The word was used in the mystery cults to describe the entry into the sanctuary. But if we take the phrase 'what he has seen' as meaning 'his visions' it does not convey any very clear meaning to speak of entering into his visions. The word is also used in the sense of entering into, or dwelling upon, a subject. This seems a more possible way of taking it. It follows on from the former phrase which speaks of the false teacher as delighting in a false humility; and now describes him further as dwelling on his visions. It may well be that there is an ironic note here in the sense that these visions are 'pseudo' in much the same way as the humility in which he delights is a hollow caricature of the real thing. C. F. D. Moule aptly sums up the commentator's problem in dealing with the phrase: 'Thus we must either take our chance of doubtful conjectural emendations, or make the best we can of the existing text.'[1]

Far from being humble, the false teacher is inflated with pride, for a religion which stems from man's speculation rather than God's revelation inevitably leads to self-esteem rather than humility. Yet this attitude of pride is utterly without justification (*vainly*), for the supposed knowledge on which it rests is not true knowledge but mere human invention. The mind which manifests such conceit is not controlled by the Spirit of God, but by the flesh. The mind of the flesh means that state in which the understanding which should rule the body is ruled by it. The phrase is virtually a synonym for the unregenerate mind, for flesh is often used, not just of the physical aspect of life, but of the nature that is unrenewed by the Spirit.

19. Once again we see the Person of Christ dominating the thoughts of this Epistle. Christ is not only the final touchstone of a man's teaching (see above, verses 8, 9), but also of the man himself. The mounting indictment reaches its climax in the accusation that the heretic does not hold fast to Christ. His hold has loosened so much that he may be classed as an apostate. To speak of a man 'not holding fast' suggests that it is not a complete outsider who is being described. It is rather one who has been outwardly numbered among the members of

[1] *Op. cit.*, p. 106.

the body, but who has never been in vital union with the Head, and whose adherence has never been the firm grasp of a true faith. The nature of this apostasy from a nominal and therefore barren attachment can be seen in contrast with the statement in Revelation ii. 13, where the firm grasp on Christ's name, even in face of persecution, is linked with a refusal to deny the faith.

The metaphor of the body is closely paralleled in Ephesians iv. 16. It is probably as unwise to press the picture too closely, as it can be undesirable to try and elicit a meaning from every detail of a parable; but certain main ideas are apparent. These are—the source of the life of the body, the growth of the body, and its unity. The source of the life of the body is Christ Himself, for He is the Head; and the phrase *from which* stresses the fact that its strength is drawn from Him. The unity of the body is divinely given (the participles are passive). Further, this unity is no mere artificial joining of parts but is a vital organic union sustained by Christ. In the parallel passage in Ephesians iv. 15, 16, the binding force is love and this would fit the context here, for 'bond' (*sundesmos*) would quite naturally suggest this thought, as we may see from Ephesians iv. 3 and Colossians iii. 14 where it is linked with peace and with love.

Then again *sumbibazō* was used earlier in the chapter (ii. 2) to convey the same idea of being 'knit together in love'. But it is important to keep the thought of unity in the context of the activity of God. Thus the ligaments and sinews[1] which join the body together are supplied (*epichorēgeō*) by Him. In the third main idea in the metaphor, the growth of the body is also set against the background of the purposes of God. The body, literally, 'increases the increase of God', that is to say, its growth is neither haphazard, nor according to any merely human pattern, but is in accordance with the plan of God. In face of any attempt to try and impose a man-made unity on the Church, or to try to develop the life of the Church by means of human expedients, it is good to return to this God-centred view of the Church, which sets it in marked contrast

[1] For details of the anatomical phraseology see Lightfoot.

to any ecclesiastical system of merely human devising; and exhibits it as the body of which Christ the Head is the source both of life and of unity; and of which God is the great architect of its growth.

20. The absurdity of the Colossians' allowing themselves to be subjected (note here the middle voice of *dogmatizō*) to a system of ritual observances is obvious, if they will but realize that in dying with Christ, they were delivered from the control of the spiritual powers of evil. To relapse then into legalism would mean that instead of being numbered with those who died with Christ and therefore live unto God (see verse 12 above), they would be like those who live with the world as their spiritual atmosphere. The contrast is between the believer who has died as far as the world is concerned, and the unregenerate man who still lives in terms of worldliness, and so is under the control of the spiritual powers of this world.

21. Such worldliness in the religious sphere manifests itself in terms of external rules—*touch not; taste not; handle not*. The AV is not quite correct in its translation, for though the verbs *haptō* and *thinganō* are virtually synonymous the former is rather stronger than the latter.[1] Hence an inversion of the order would be truer to the meaning—'handle not, taste not, touch not'. This descending order also brings out more forcibly the scrupulous legalism of the heretics. They not only forbid handling what is unclean, but even touching it. The suggestion that handling (*haptō*) refers here to a prohibition as regards marriage is possible, but not very probable. In the first place, such a major issue would hardly be dismissed so easily by Paul. Then again, the context points rather to ceremonial uncleanness in terms of meats and drinks which perish in the using, and marriage would scarcely fit into this scheme.

22. The pointlessness of ceremonial prohibition is demonstrated by the temporary nature of the very things which are

[1] Trench, *New Testament Synonyms*, p. 56.

forbidden. They belong to this world whereas the believer belongs to eternity. How absurd then to subject himself to material ordinances which have no abiding reality. Thus, Paul insists, all these things, i.e. these foods and drinks which have been forbidden by the ritualists, are destined for corruption. The phrase is literally 'with a view to corruption with the using'; and the meaning would seem to be that these things are designed to be destroyed as they are used. They are essentially a part of the corruptible order of this world, and therefore cannot bind the believer.

Paul resumes after the brief parenthesis with a renewed emphasis that these ordinances are not divinely given, but spring rather from the precepts and instructions of men. The two words are linked closely into one phrase which covers both the authority with which these precepts are given, and the body of teaching by which they are conveyed. The phrase recalls the LXX of Isaiah xxix. 13 quoted in Matthew xv. 9 and Mark vii. 7. Commenting on the latter passage H. B. Swete suggests that the use of the plural perhaps points to the multiplicity of details and the absence of an underlying principle.

23. In this most difficult verse various suggested interpretations have been advanced; but the most likely are those represented by the RV, the AV and the RSV margin. As against the AV which takes *flesh* as equivalent to 'body' we might note that in this verse they are set in contrast; and also that *flesh* has been used in its idiomatic or ethical sense in verse 13. Another objection is that the word translated *satisfying*, *plēsmonē*, which appears only here in biblical Greek, has the meaning elsewhere of satiety (see Lightfoot), and Paul would hardly set as an ideal, even in contrast to asceticism, an excessive indulgence of the body. The RV interpretation, on the other hand, faces the objection that it imposes an unusual meaning on the preposition *pros* by making it mean 'against'. One further possibility which does justice to the juxtaposition of body and flesh, and also to the normal usage of *pros*, would be to take *not in any honour* in an absolute sense and to read with the RSV margin 'are of no value, serving only to indulge the flesh'. Olshausen has a similar view, and suggests that *body* should be understood after *honour*. The meaning then would be that asceticism does not do honour to the body, but only promotes the indulgence of the flesh.

The suggestions of the RSV margin or of Olshausen also seem to fit the total context of the verse. Paul is reaching the climax of his argument in which he is denying to these man-made doctrines any real value. It is true that they have an appearance of wisdom. To a superficial observer a body of doctrines which shows itself in a form of worship, in an apparent humility, and in asceticism, might seem to be the doctrines of wise men; but this religious devotion is self-imposed (the words forming the compound *ethelothrēskeia* imply a form of worship which a man devises for himself). The humility, as Paul has shown earlier (verse 18), is affected, and is far removed from true humility. The ascetic attitude stems from a mistaken view of the sinfulness of the body as such, and thus does no honour to the body which God intends us to reverence. And all these, Paul insists, whatever *shew of wisdom* they may have, are of no real value, but, by pandering to human pride, only tend to the indulgence of the old sinful nature.

V. A NEW PATTERN OF LIFE (iii. 1–iv. 1)

a. New aims for new men (iii. 1–4)

1, 2. It is typical of Paul that having laid a doctrinal foundation he proceeds to erect an ethical superstructure. Hence we have the transition here from theological statement to practical precept. The Christian, he says, has experienced a radical change of spiritual environment and this should affect his whole mode of life. Having been raised with Christ he now moves in a new sphere. This should mean that he has a new aim in life. Normal human ambition is in terms of this world. But the one who has been raised with Christ sees things from an eternal perspective, and so should aim that his life on earth should be dominated by the pattern of life seen in the glorified

Christ. The *right hand of God* is the place of holiness, of intercession and of power. Hence to *seek those things which are above* is to aim at emulating the characteristics of the Christ of glory. Thus growth in holiness, depth in prayer, and advance in spiritual power should be the aims which fill the believer's horizon.

He should also have a new attitude of mind. In face of the constant battle with temptation at the level of the thought-life, the believer must not only resist evil thoughts, but positively set his thoughts on the things of God. The things of earth are at best temporary. Thus it is vanity and vexation of spirit to set his thoughts on things which are fleeting. The *things above* are eternal, so there is a depth of quality and an abiding value which merits the concentration of his mind upon them.

3, 4. The reason for this call to the right kind of heavenly-mindedness is the fact that, in Christ, the believer has died to the world. Before, he was dead as far as God was concerned. But now that the miracle of spiritual regeneration has taken place he is alive unto God, but dead as far as the world and its mode of life is concerned.

It is true, to be sure, that this new life is hidden from view. The world does not see this new life which the believer has experienced, and, as a result, misunderstanding, enmity, and scorn are the believer's lot. But this hidden life will be vindicated. Just as Christ is hidden from all but the eyes of faith, so this life is hidden in the secret counsels of God. Indeed God Himself is the very element in which this life moves. He is not only the author of it; He is its constant source of support and supply. But the day of vindication will dawn. The Christ, who is now ignored or rejected by the world, will be revealed in a blaze of glory in which the full splendour of His divine Being will be seen. But Christ is our very life. It is not only that He is its source, but He lives in us, so that our new life is really His life in us. There is thus an organic spiritual unity between the believer and his Lord. Hence in the day when

Christ is revealed, the life of the Christian, long despised or ignored by the world, will also be revealed as something which eternally abides when the temporary things of this world are doomed to destruction.

b. Mortifying the old nature (iii. 5-11)

5. The *therefore* of verse 5 points to what has gone before. It is because Christ is his life that the believer is called, not to an unavailing struggle in his own strength, but to one in dependence on the power of the glorified Lord. Further, the prospect just mentioned of the glory that lies ahead should be an incentive to the Christian to prepare for that day. This will involve a resolute putting to death of the old nature. But has not Paul already said that the believer has died? True, but this is from the ideal standpoint. He died to sin in the sense that sin forfeited any claim upon him; but this ideal status must be wrought out in terms of practical experience. By constantly turning his back on self and turning in submission to Christ, he must realize experimentally what, from the viewpoint of eternity, is an accomplished fact.

The Christian is a new man, but he is still in the body and so has to contend with the old nature, designated earlier as the 'flesh'. The limbs of the body may therefore be either instruments of the old nature or of the new man. The body may be the avenue by which temptation is admitted, or it may become, by the grace of God, the temple of the Holy Spirit. Paul therefore uses a vigorous metaphor, and calls for a slaying of the limbs of the body. The body in so far as it becomes earth-bound is to be dealt with radically. Any activity or tendency of the body which makes it subject to the old nature calls for mortification in the sense of determined refusal to yield to its appeal. For a similar call, compare Matthew xviii. 8 ff. If we take the words which follow, as being in apposition to *members*, we have some of the vicious activities of the flesh which are to be repudiated. *Fornication* speaks of sexual immorality, while *uncleanness* adds the note of perversion, as may be seen from Romans i. 24. But such sins are not only in terms of outward action, but also of the underlying lust. Thus the passion which desires what is illicit, and indeed every kind of evil desire, is also forbidden—there seems to be a movement in thought here from the particular to the more general.

It is hard to resist the suggestion that *covetousness* is linked here with sexual immorality; and so speaks of the greed which seeks its satisfaction in what is not lawful. Thus, in Ephesians iv. 19 and v. 5 it is also linked with impurity, while in 1 Thessalonians iv. 6, Paul uses the cognate verb to describe adultery as a defrauding of one's neighbour by possessing that which is especially his. This sin is idolatrous, for it concentrates the whole being upon something other than God. It is characteristic of sexual indulgence that it leads to an unhealthy, and ultimately perverted, obsession. This can be seen not only on an individual level, but also in a community. When godliness is rejected, and the lust of the flesh encouraged, it is not long before sex is worshipped instead of God.

6, 7. A warning is added, based on the fact of God's judgment on sinners. The present tense *cometh* suggests that judgment is not a future event but a present reality. C. F. D. Moule tries to argue that *wrath* should be rendered as 'disaster', which would mean that Paul is not describing so much the activity of God Himself, as the outworking of an impersonal moral principle. But in Romans i it is quite clear in the repeated usage of the phrase 'God gave them up' that Paul has in mind the direct personal activity of God Himself. Thus God does not stand as a spectator viewing the consequences which man's sin brings upon him; but rather intervenes in a judgment which may manifest itself in leaving men to wallow in the filth of their own lusts, so that they are worthy objects of the final condemnation.[1]

Lightfoot urges that in spite of the overwhelming MS attestation in favour of the retention of the phrase 'upon the sons of disobedience', it should be omitted. His objection

[1] See Leon Morris, *op. cit.*, pp. 161 ff.

is that it is so like the parallel in Ephesians v. 6 that the suspicion of copying is strong. He adds that on exegetical grounds it is better to read 'in which' instead of 'among whom'. But in reply we might point out that apart from the very strong evidence in favour of the phrase, from the vast majority of the authorities, there is the further consideration that such a phrase seems required to complete the sense. Then, too, the emphasis on *ye also*, verse 7, implies a contrast with those who have lived in disobedience. If we retain the phrase it would seem best to take the two relative pronouns as being masculine and neuter respectively, and render them 'among whom' and 'in these'. The sense will then be that they once walked in company with unbelievers and also partook of their sins.

8. *But now* that you have been raised with Christ, says Paul, you must exhibit a totally different attitude to sin. No longer is it your natural environment. It is rather something to be 'put away' as one discards filthy rags. *Anger* speaks of the settled attitude, while *wrath* is the passionate outburst. It is rather unfortunate that the AV should render the same word, *orgē*, in verse 6 as 'wrath' and in verse 8 as *anger*. It is surely significant that Paul can speak in the same context of the wrath of God as an inevitable moral consequence of His character, while the wrath of man is sinful because it springs from his fallen nature. This meets the objection of those who deny the biblical conception of the wrath of God because they think it implies a vindictiveness which is unworthy of God's character. Yet here such vindictiveness must only be predicated of man whose *wrath* is therefore sinful in essence. The word translated *malice*, *kakia*, is a general one for wickedness. In the context here, where the emphasis is on speech, it probably refers to malicious gossip. *Blasphemy*, which is more often used in relation to God, is here obviously used rather in relation to men. It refers to abusive words or slander directed against another. Foul talk likewise is to be avoided; and this covers not only obscenity, but also the innuendoes and suggestive expressions which cover an underlying impurity. The phrase *out of your mouth* can scarcely be simply a statement of the source of the foul talk. It would then be redundant, for it would be explaining what is obvious. It seems rather to point back to the verb *put off* at the beginning of the verse. These sins are to be put away from their lips. This confirms the impression that the vices here denounced, while they may refer to attitudes of mind, have a primary reference to the spoken word.

9, 10. We are still moving in the sphere of sins of the tongue, as lying is forbidden. Whether it be a deliberate untruth, or the half truth which conveys a wrong impression, or the exaggeration which distorts the facts, all these savour of the old unregenerate nature rather than of the new. But they have *put off* like soiled clothes *the old man* and have *put on* the new. By *the old man* he means the man they were in Adam. By *the new man* Paul means the man they are in Christ. The believer has ceased to be what he once was. As a new creature in Christ he can never be the same. Hence the practices which were normal to him in his unregenerate state are now completely unnatural. The new man is continually being renewed by God; and this renewal aims at a growth in knowledge. It is a characteristic of the old man that while the conscience still functions, it is impaired because the facts upon which the conscience must base its decision are themselves unreliable, in that they are the product of spiritual ignorance. Thus, if conscience is to function properly, there must be a renewal of moral and spiritual discernment. When God first created man He created him in His own image. This meant that man was a moral being with a clear understanding of right and wrong, and the ability to choose. That condition, which was forfeited by the fall, now becomes the pattern according to which God re-fashions the new nature of the believer, which is the new creation.

11. In this new sphere in which the regenerate man moves, the divisions which are accepted as normal and inevitable by the natural man, cease to be applicable. It may be, as Lightfoot suggests, that Paul introduces this thought to deal a blow at the Judaism of Colossae which distinguished Jew and Greek; and also at the Gnosticism which set the learned Greek over against the unlearned, while the problem of Onesimus the runaway slave leads him to add the further reference to bond and free. Another possibility is that he is simply developing the thought of the previous verse. The sins which are forbidden (8, 9) are essentially those which spring from division, and involve a lack of respect for the personality of the one against whom the offence is committed. This spirit of divisiveness and hatred showed itself on a large scale in the ancient world in the religious, cultural, and social barriers which divided nation from nation, and man from man. But, for the regenerate man, while these distinctions exist as a fact of experience, they have no real significance, and certainly no religious sanction.

Greek and *Jew* spoke of the great religious division which Judaism still sought to perpetuate. The following terms *circumcision* and *uncircumcision* might appear to be mere repetition; but are more likely intended to cover those who had become proselytes to Judaism and thus inherited the antipathy to those who may have been of the same race but were marked as religiously different because they were uncircumcised. *Barbarian* and *Scythian* can hardly be a contrast. The former term to Greek minds would suggest a foreigner who was an alien to Greek culture, while the latter would suggest an even more primitive state, and to Jews with memories from their own history of the savagery of the Scythian invasion of the eighth century BC, it would convey a similar impression. Both terms would therefore seem to be an extension of the category 'uncircumcised' to the utmost limit. Even the most primitive or savage people are capable of being drawn within the orbit of the redeemed. *Bond* and *free* cover the other major division which was not only economic but social.

All these petty distinctions are shown to be of no ultimate importance once it is seen that Christ is everything, and dwells *in all*, i.e. in all His people whatever their race or background.

To say that Christ *is all*, is to assert that He so dominates the whole order of being that persons and things have significance, not so much in their relation to each other, as in their relation to Him. But there is no absorption of personality as in the conception of an Absolute which embraces all being in itself, for the Christ who *is all* dwells *in all* who retain their distinctiveness yet find a unity in Him. In a world still bitterly divided by race, colour and social status, and in which the Church too easily succumbs to conventional attitudes, here is a truth which needs to be constantly recalled.

c. Putting on the new (iii. 12-17)

12. The counterpart to the rejection of the rags of the old nature is the decisive putting on (note the aorist) of the garments of righteousness. This command is no legalistic requirement, for it is set in the context of the Colossians' status as God's people. It is this status which is the incentive to holy living. The words which describe them as the people of God recall Old Testament usage. They are the covenant people, the new Israel. They are *the elect of God* in that He has chosen them from among men, and chosen them for Himself so that being separate from the world they might be *holy* unto the Lord. Thus we can see the close connection between 'elect' and 'holy', which suggests that the words *holy and beloved* are not to be taken as vocatives, but rather as in apposition to *elect* which they amplify. *Beloved*, then, is not here used as a term of affection by Paul, but rather stresses the fact that they as the chosen people have been made the objects of God's love. This deepens the motive for that love of the brethren which is here being enjoined. It is a similar thought to that of 1 John iv. 11, 'Beloved, if God so loved us, we ought also to love one another.'

The virtues to which they are to aspire may be grouped as they are viewed from different aspects. They deal with a believer's treatment of others, with his estimate of himself, and with his reaction to his treatment by others. As far as his attitude to others is concerned, he is to display mercy not just at the level of a forgiving attitude, but with the further note of an inner yearning which feels deeply for another. *Kindness* similarly speaks of the desire for another's good. As to his own estimate of himself, the believer is to be humble. This will affect his attitude to others, for it is only the man who sees himself as the object of God's mercy and who acknowledges that he has no rights to assert, who will be patient with others. Thus, *humbleness of mind* leads on to *meekness* and *longsuffering*. *Meekness* is here used primarily with reference to men rather than to God, though it is true that the former presupposes the latter. It means a spirit of quiet submission as exemplified in Christ, who did not insist on His own rights or comforts but submitted to the will of God. So it means, in the context of relationship with others, a readiness to give way when no principle is at stake but only some personal opinion or desire. It does not imply weakness but rather Christian courtesy. *Longsuffering* is the response in face of provocation. It is the resolute refusal to retaliate, in contrast to the natural reaction of the unregenerate man.

13. The importance of these last virtues is seen in the emphasis given by the explanatory parenthesis which follows. Olshausen suggests that the disputes due to the false teachers may have called forth bitterness; hence the added stress on forbearance. The believers are to bear with others and they are to forgive any injuries or slights received. This forgiveness is to be extended graciously even though the recipient may be unworthy (for the meaning of *charizomai* see above on ii. 13). Thus the pattern is the gracious forgiveness of Christ. There is a subtle variation in the pronouns which introduces a further shade of meaning. They are to bear with *one another*, *allēlōn*, with a reciprocity which affects all the individuals in the fellowship. They are literally 'to forgive themselves', *heautois*, where the emphasis is on the corporate nature of the fellowship to which this spirit of forgiveness belongs. Thus Alford comments: ' "Forgiving yourselves", did it not convey to our ears a wrong idea, would be the best rendering; doing as a body, for yourselves, that which God did once for you all.'

Thus, even if there is a reasonable cause for complaint (*a quarrel*), this does not justify a refusal to forgive, for the Lord had assuredly a just cause for complaint against us because of our rebellion, and yet in free grace has extended His forgiveness.

14. The metaphor of putting on clothes continues as Paul exhorts them to put on love above all those virtues which they have already donned. But love is no mere additional garment. It is not one more virtue to be added to the list. Indeed, it is not only the supreme virtue (for this would leave the others as it were independent); it is rather the bond which knits all the others together and gives completeness. It seems most inadequate to interpret *bond of perfectness* merely as the 'perfect bond'. It means rather the bond which brings perfection or completeness. It is love which is the life-blood of the other virtues. Without love they are only dutiful moral attitudes, but with love they are blended into a moral unity which is complete. Completeness would also suggest the idea of being acceptable to God. Thus Paul earlier spoke of his aim to present each believer 'perfect' (*teleios*) before God (i. 28). Love, then, makes all the other virtues acceptable to God. Alford sees in the use of the definite article before love (*tēn agapēn*) an allusion to the specific, well-known love which should characterize the Christian.

15. *The peace of God*—or rather, as a better attested reading, 'the peace of Christ'—is that peace which Christ gives. Peace here is being employed in the subjective sense as an inner state, rather than in its objective usage as a harmonious relationship with God, though of course the former depends on the latter. But peace is not only Christ's gift, but also His desire for the believer, for it is to peace that they have been called. It would seem also, in spite of the opinion of various commentators, that *peace* is not here being applied primarily to that inner harmony which reigns when conflicts and tensions have been resolved. It is rather inner peace as far as the attitude of mind and will towards others is concerned. Thus it is set in the context of social virtues. It follows on 'love' of which, indeed, it is the outworking. It is a call to those who have been knit together *in one body*. All this confirms the view that it is the attitude of the believer to others which is still under consideration. Peace is to act as an umpire. The verb here translated *rule*, *brabeuō*, would describe the activity of the umpire in the games, who decides the contest. Thus in the inner conflict which would inevitably accompany many of their attitudes, when love and bitterness contend for the mastery, peace is to be the governing factor. Membership in the one body of Christ involves a call to maintain peace among the members. Each member therefore must himself be governed by this inner desire for peace, and this peace is Christ's gift.

Closely allied to this peaceable disposition is a spirit of thanksgiving. This may have a twofold reference; for, while thanksgiving is primarily due to God for all His mercies, a ready gratitude towards men will also make for peace. Thanksgiving towards God will beget humility, for it develops the awareness that every gift is from Him, and so it deals a blow at the self-opinionated attitude which breeds scorn of others. Similarly, by turning the thoughts away towards God, it kills self-pity which is the parent of resentment and bitterness. In this context, thanksgiving may stem from an awareness of the privilege of being called to membership in the body of Christ, which will lead to a determination to live worthy of such a privilege. In all these cases a spirit of humble gratitude to God has its effect on relationships with men. But there may also be the thought that thanksgiving should also characterize our attitude to others. To be grateful to men will mean being constantly alert to discern in their words and deeds any possible ground for gratitude, rather than being on the watch for an encroachment on our rights which must be resisted.

16. The punctuation of this verse presents a problem. Are we to follow the AV and take *in all wisdom* with what precedes, or should it be taken with what follows? Should *teaching and admonishing* be taken with *psalms and hymns*? It is hard to decide, but the parallels in i. 28 and Ephesians v. 18, 19 would suggest that we should include *in all wisdom* with the phrase which follows, and then follow the AV for the remainder of the verse. This also does justice to the balance of the phrase: *in all wisdom teaching . . . with grace singing, en pasē sophia didaskontes . . . en chariti adontes.*

The word of Christ may mean that spoken by Christ, or spoken of Christ. In either case it still points to the revealed word, the word of the gospel. This word is to have its settled abode in the hearts of Christians so that there is a submission to its demands. The context here however makes the application not so much personal, as corporate. It is in the body of believers that the word is to *dwell*, though there is of course ultimately a personal reference involved in this, for the indwelling is not among them in the sense merely of being a common possession, but 'in them' as a truth inwardly received. The word indwells *richly* when its fullness is received. There must not be contentment with a spiritual pittance, for all the wealth of the word must be their desire. As a result, the word will be rich in its outcome. It will be the means of leading them into spiritual wealth.

Their experience of the word is not a merely individual one, for it is in the context of the fellowship of the Church that they are to learn its truths. Thus there must be a mutual sharing of the word. It is from the indwelling word that they will learn the wisdom of God, and that wisdom will then become the atmosphere in which they move as they seek to build one another up in knowledge. The worship of the Church is here viewed from the standpoint of the edification of the believers. Lightfoot suggests, admittedly rather tentatively, that *psalms* refers to the psalms of David inherited from the synagogue worship, *hymns* to specifically Christian compositions, while the more general term *songs* refers to any form of musical expression which can be qualified by the term *spiritual*. Such singing will not be a mere form of release, but will be a means of instruction. This instruction is viewed from two angles. *Teaching* will refer to the positive imparting of precepts; while *admonishing* introduces the negative element, and the note of warning. If the public worship in the church is to fulfil this task, there must be certain vital elements in it; and they are seen here. The singing must be rooted in the word. It is against the background of the indwelling word that this exhortation to edifying praise is set. True hymnody must be doctrinal in content. It must be rendered *with grace*. Calvin interprets this as simply meaning 'graciously' or 'acceptably', and C. F. D. Moule suggests 'gratefully singing'. If, however (reading *en tē chariti*), we do justice to the definite article, there will be a reference here to the grace of God. The grace will be the sphere in which the worshipper moves. His singing will be the outward expression of his inner experience of God's grace— he will sing 'in the grace'. Then again, praise must come from the heart, not only in the sense of expressing the true aspirations of the worshipper, but also because the truths implicit in such *spiritual songs* will require an inner reflection and assent. Finally it must be offered *to the Lord*. This guards against the possibility of their imagining that because the worship should be edifying, therefore this is its chief function. Its primary reference is God-ward and its edifying work is an outcome. Indeed, the more its God-ward aspect is kept in view, the more will the believers be built up as their minds and hearts are drawn towards Him.

17. This verse is primarily a general summary of the pre- ceding verses, but ultimately its basis is the main theme of the Epistle, namely the pre-eminence of Christ. His sovereignty embraces every aspect of life, not only the so-called 'sacred' but also the secular. To *do all in the name of the Lord Jesus* means to live and act as those who bear His name, and so to seek to live worthy of Him. It means also to act as those for whom He is Lord, and this involves obedience to His will. It means reliance upon Him, for the name speaks of the person, and to speak of acting 'in the name' is to use a phrase very much akin to the familiar usage 'in Christ', 'in the Lord', etc. There is however no hint that such a life of obedience is to be conceived in terms of duty, but rather of 'thanksgiving'. This steady attitude of thanksgiving (note the present participle *eucharestountes*) breathes the spirit of childlike dependence as it is offered to God the Father. Finally, Christ who is the goal of their living is to be the medium of their thanksgiving which is to be offered *by him*.

d. Practical injunctions (iii. 18—iv. 1)

18, 19. The recurrence of the significant phrase *in the Lord* is a reminder that, for the believer, human relationships must be considered from the standpoint of this basic relationship with Christ. The submission of the wife to the husband is befitting to those who are *in the Lord*, and who thus accept the divine pattern as seen in the original design of the Creator. But the emphasis in this series of injunctions for the family is that responsibilities are reciprocal. If the wife offers obedience it is in the context of the husband's love. There must be no self-seeking on the husband's part, for Christian love (*agapē*), as exemplified supremely in Christ, is far removed from mere natural love (*erōs*) in that it seeks primarily the good of the beloved rather than the satisfaction to be gained from the relationship. Negatively the husband is warned of the danger of petty tyranny when bitterness or harshness usurps the place of love.

20, 21. The obedience which children are to yield is not qualified to make provision for the problem of commands which are contrary to conscience. This however is covered by the fact that the whole relationship is subject to the Lord. The main issue here is that the obedience is total. It is to be governed, not by the child's wishes, but by the very fact of his position as a child. This obedience is acceptable in the sphere where the Lordship of Christ is the paramount consideration. But again there is a complementary responsibility. If children must yield unquestioning obedience, then the parent must be on his guard lest he discourage the child by unreasonable demands, by the brusqueness of his approach, by humiliating his child before others, or by any other failure to treat the child with understanding. Over-severity can so crush the spirit that the child loses heart in the unequal struggle. Bengel aptly comments that a broken-down spirit is the bane of youth.

The relatively fuller treatment accorded to the relationship of masters and slaves (**iii. 22–iv. 1**) as compared with that given to husbands and wives may well be due to issues raised by the runaway slave Onesimus, the subject of the Epistle to Philemon, and the companion of the bearer of this Epistle. Paul was always anxious to avoid giving the wrong impression (witness, e.g., his concern over financial matters at Corinth); and it would therefore be natural that he should guard against the suggestion that his appeal on behalf of Onesimus in any way condoned the latter's wrongdoing, or justified a break-down in the social order. In addition, it was obvious that in a slave-society it was imperative that the position of slaves in the Church be made clear, and the duties of Christian masters should also be outlined.

There are some general principles to be noted in Paul's treatment of this issue. The overriding consideration is the Lordship of Christ, which transforms the quality of the service rendered, and also encourages the slave in face of harsh treatment, while at the same time it curbs the tendency of the master to be unduly oppressive. Then it is also noteworthy that in contrast to prevailing practice Paul treats the slaves as persons, not as things. In the world of the first century the slave was a chattel, little different from a beast of burden and therefore with no civic or other rights. But Paul's emphasis that the slave is a person can be seen in the first place in that he addresses them as responsible members of the Church. Indeed the fact that he does not merely issue commands and pro-hibitions but gives explanations presupposes that those addressed are capable of understanding and of moral choice. The third general principle is that of reciprocity which we have already noted above. The demand for complete obedience is paralleled by a demand for fair dealing by the master.

22, 23. Applying the Lordship of Christ to the situation of the slave Paul reminds them that their masters are *according to the flesh*. This does not involve any lessening of their authority, but it sets that authority in its right perspective as being subject to Christ's sovereignty. If Christ is Lord, then the quality of their service must be such as will please Him. *Eyeservice* is the rendering of the barest minimum, or perhaps the carrying out of a duty without having any real interest in doing so. This superficial service is linked with the word *menpleasers* which has an unworthy ring in view of the Christian's primary loyalty to please his Lord. His attitude to his work should rather be governed by the fear of the Lord, that reverential awe for his God. This fear will mean that his duties will be done with an upright heart. *Singleness of heart, en haplotēti kardias*, translates in the LXX the Hebrew *bᵉyosher lᵉbabi* in I Chronicles xxix. 17, and speaks of a heart which is so true that it will bear God's scrutiny. True service will spring from within (*heartily*, lit. 'from the soul') and will be directed ultimately towards the Lord.

24. The Lordship of Christ is also a means of encouragement and an incentive to faithful service. They may receive nothing from their earthly masters but abuse and ill-treatment, but there is a Master who will reward. Lightfoot stresses the absence of the article before master which is 'the more remarkable because it is studiously inserted in the context vv. 22–24'. Men may treat them as chattels but God treats them as sons and indeed as heirs (see also above on i. 12). Here, incidentally, as Calvin points out, is an answer to the Roman Catholic attempt to find in this a justification for a doctrine of works and rewards. *The reward* consists of *the inheritance*, but this is due to the grace of God who has adopted them. The pledge of this reward is Christ Himself. The order of the words brings this out. We might render: 'It is the Lord Christ that you serve.'

25. It is difficult to decide if *he that doeth wrong* refers to the slave or the master, and indeed Lightfoot suggests that it has reference to both. The context however would lead us to suppose that it refers to the unjust master. The *but, gar,* links it to the preceding sentence. There Paul was dealing with the slave facing oppressive treatment, and spoke of the slave's reward. Now he turns to the other aspect, and speaks of the requital given to the unrighteous master by the Lord who has *no respect of persons,* but acts with complete impartiality.

iv. 1. Having spoken at length on the relationship the apostle only adds a brief but pointed command to the masters. It immediately follows the reminder that God is no respecter of persons, and it reiterates the main theme of the Lordship of Christ. Masters as well as slaves are alike subject to the Lord. Treatment of slaves must be *just (dikaios).* The frequent usage of this word and its cognates in the New Testament to describe a man's acceptance by God would suggest here the thought that it is not enough that their treatment should conform to the conventional morality of the community; but that it should be acceptable to God. It should also be *equal.* There should be fairness in the attitude. This involves the thought that in a sense the master has a debt to his slave which he must discharge as before their common Lord.

VI. FINAL INSTRUCTIONS (iv. 2-6)

a. The duty of prayer (iv. 2-4)

2. To *continue in prayer* is not merely to maintain a habit. There is the note of diligence and persistence, for this is a task from which a man is easily deflected. This thought is developed by the mention of watchfulness. This affects not only prayer itself but also the manner in which it is offered. Watchfulness suggests a danger to be avoided and this danger comes from two main quarters. The evil one makes the believer careless, so that he neglects the very practice of prayer, or on the other hand he dulls his mind or distracts his thoughts. Hence watchfulness means a disciplined attention to this continuous ministry, and it also involves a concentration of the whole being on its discharge. *Thanksgiving* is mentioned as the characteristic element in prayer to which Paul constantly reverts, but also, surely, because praise imparts a spiritual freshness to prayer which acts as an antidote to that sluggishness of soul which he is here seeking to combat.

3, 4. The request that God *would open unto us a door of utterance* may be taken in two ways. Some, e.g. Lightfoot, Abbott, C. F. D. Moule, take it as a desire that the obstacles in the way of the preaching of the gospel might be removed, and that a door of opportunity might be opened. There might also be a hint of Paul's desire, expressed in Philemon 22, that he might be released; for this would obviously open the door for a much wider apostolic ministry. This is a possible interpretation, and its strength lies in the citation of similar passages (e.g. 1 Cor. xvi. 9; 2 Cor. ii. 12). On the other hand, it may be viewed as a desire that he may be given by the Spirit that ability to preach the gospel which is beyond the unaided natural powers. In favour of this is the closely parallel passage in Ephesians vi. 19, 20 where it is quite clear that it is the opening of the mouth that is involved. This position is strengthened by the change of the pronoun from the first person plural to the first person singular. Had he been thinking of freedom, he might well have prayed that the door might be opened for him to preach. But he includes in this prayer those who were free like Timothy, Epaphras and the others. Their freedom however did not mean that they could preach easily. Such freedom constantly required God's help. Thus, whether it were they with their liberty or Paul with his bonds, all required prayer. Incidentally, here is a reply to Masson who sees here the hand of the interpolator (the author of Ephesians) who is responsible for the second part of the verse. After all Paul can quite easily thus move from the plural to the singular as in 2 Corinthians i, ii, xiii.

b. The duty of witness (iv. 5, 6)

5. Their regular intercourse with unbelievers is to be governed by *wisdom*. This is no mere human wisdom but comes from above. Indeed, as Paul has already stated, Christ is the source of this wisdom, and so, as the believer is in Christ, he is in touch with the wisdom which can guide his steps. He is to redeem the time. *Redeeming* may be used in the sense of 'make the most of'. The thought would be that in view of the shortness of the time, because of the Parousia, every opportunity must be bought up. But the parallel passage in Ephesians, coupled with the fact that there is no allusion here to the Parousia, suggests that the AV is possibly nearer to the true interpretation. Evil days are those in which the power of the devil is being manifested. Even for the believer, days which should be used for the glory of God are all too easily relinquished to the evil one. He must therefore regain for fruitful use the days which the devil would misuse.

6. Consistency of life must be followed by the witness of the spoken word. It hardly seems adequate, in view of Paul's high view of grace, to see here merely an allusion to a gracious or acceptable way of speaking. This is of course true, but there is much more in the phrase 'in grace' (*en chariti*). *Grace* is, as it were, the element in which the believer moves. He speaks as one who has experienced, and indeed constantly experiences, the grace of God. This should influence the content of his words as he seeks to avoid what would be unworthy of the God who has saved him, and to impart continually that which will edify the hearer. It should beget a spirit of humility, for one who is himself a debtor to grace can scarcely be boastful before men. It should lead to a gracious approach, for an awareness of God's merciful dealings with him should deliver him from a brusque or ungracious attitude to others.

The meaning of the phrase *seasoned with salt* will be governed by the words which follow. It is in order that the believer may know how to answer those who question him that he is to season his conversation. Food is seasoned in order to make it appetizing; similarly, the Christian must live so constantly in the atmosphere of the grace of God that his words will be palatable to those he meets. But if such speech is to be really wholesome, it will mean that it must be free from corruption. He will exchange the filthy conversation of the world which corrupts both speaker and hearer for the word which is pure and edifying. A similar injunction is seen in Ephesians iv. 29.

VII. PERSONAL GREETINGS (iv. 7–18)

7, 8. There is a close parallel with Ephesians vi. 21, 22, where *Tychicus* is also the bearer of the letter. He is being sent not merely to take the letter to them but to let them know of Paul's affairs and so to strengthen their hearts. It seems quite clear that the better reading is that which lies behind the RV 'that ye may know our estate' (RSV, 'that you may know how we are'). To take the reading of the Received Text, which underlies the AV *that he might know your estate*, would be to miss the point of what Paul is saying. He has stated in verse 7 what Tychicus will do, and adds by way of explanation that he has sent him 'for this very purpose' (RV). Quite clearly this purpose must be parallel to that which he has stated in the previous verse. The MS evidence confirms the argument drawn from the context against the received reading. What is said of Tychicus shows the high esteem in which he is held. The three-fold description is closely knit together, and it would therefore seem best to take the phrase *in the Lord* as qualifying all three expressions. It is because of his union with Christ that he has these other relationships. He is a *brother* to them all, and by his character has merited the title *beloved*. He is a servant of the church, and he is a *fellowservant* (lit. 'a fellow slave')—the link envisaged being doubtless with Paul himself.

9. *Onesimus*, himself the subject of the letter to Philemon, is accompanying Tychicus who is bearing these two letters and the letter 'to the Ephesians'.[1] It is noteworthy that Paul does not apply words of commendation indiscriminately. Thus while he speaks in terms similar to those which he had used of

---

[1] See note on iv. 15 below.

Tychicus, of Onesimus' new status as a believer, describing him as one who has already proved faithful and become a beloved brother, yet he does not speak of his Christian service as he did in the case of Tychicus. It is a striking comment on how the apostle's thought has leapt across the barriers of social distinction, that he can describe the runaway slave as *one of you*, a phrase which he will use presently of the highly honoured Epaphras.

10. *Aristarchus* was associated with Paul in the riot of Ephesus (Acts xix. 29). It may be that a recollection of this incident prompts the use of the title *fellowprisoner*. But, if physical imprisonment is meant, a more natural explanation would be that Aristarchus was already in some way sharing Paul's imprisonment at Rome. It seems, however, that the reference here is to a spiritual bondage. Thus it is applied to Aristarchus here but not to Epaphras, while in Philemon it is the latter who is accorded the title. Since the letters reflect a common situation such a difference would be inexplicable unless he is referring to the bondage of Christ. The conjecture noted by Abbott that they possibly took turns in sharing the imprisonment is rather forced.

11. Paul obviously does not mean by *these only* that the Gentile believers, whose names will follow, were not also fellow-workers (see Phm. 24). He is rather singling out these Jewish Christians from the rest of the circumcision party from whom he always met opposition. There is an incidental reference to Paul's affectionate nature as he speaks of the help of those who had been *a comfort* to him in his affliction.

12. The description of the passionate earnestness in prayer of *Epaphras* recalls Paul's own spirit of prayer of which he spoke earlier, and also the burden of his prayer that they might be spiritually mature (i. 29, ii. 1). It is difficult to decide how to interpret the word *complete* which the RV translates 'fully assured'. The word *plērophoreō* is used in the New Testament

99

both in the sense of 'to assure fully' (Rom. iv. 21, xiv. 5) or 'to fulfil' (2 Tim. iv. 5, 17). The following factors seem to favour the AV translation. The meaning of the word is partly determined by the way we take the phrase which follows, *in all the will of God*. It would be possible to link this with the verb *ye may stand*, but it seems more natural to take it with the participle which immediately precedes. If this is so then the more likely meaning of this participle is 'fulfilled', for this not only completes the parallel with *perfect* (*teleioi*) but also accords with Paul's earlier usage (i. 9) when he prays that 'ye might be filled with the knowledge of his will'. The meaning would then be that their spiritual experience will be filled out to completeness through their knowledge and performance of the complete will of God. Thus Chrysostom comments: 'It is not enough, simply to do His will. He that is filled, suffereth not any other will to be within him, for if so, he is not wholly filled.'

13. Instead of *zeal* we should read with the best MS authorities 'pain' (*ponon*). The word is used in the Apocalypse (xvi. 10, 11, xxi. 4) and can speak of intense pain. It is thus an apt word to use here for the spiritual travail involved in prayer, which he has already described as 'labouring'.

14. Lightfoot suggests that the absence of any epithet with the name of *Demas* may foreshadow his later failure when Luke stood firm (2 Tim. iv. 10). Indeed we may without forcing the greeting see the possible reason for his failure. Both here and in Philemon 24 he is only a name linked with Luke. Was he one of those who are carried forward by the momentum of another's faith, but whose own faith is too shallow to endure the demands of a major test?

15, 16. The truths which Paul has been declaring in this Epistle are not only for the church in Colossae but have a wider scope. So the Epistle is to be sent to the larger city of *Laodicea*. Here we see in germ the conception of the Scriptures as being not only messages for a given situation but as having reference to the whole Church of God. This sharing of the apostolic message was to be mutual, for the church in Laodicea which met in the house of *Nymphas* and his family (read 'their' house) also had a letter which they in turn were to pass on to the believers in Colossae. There have been very many suggestions as to the identity of this letter and Lightfoot has an extended note on the various theories.[1] We can dismiss the extant apocryphal letter to the Laodiceans which is late in origin, and which probably had its birth in an attempt to supply a letter to fit the demands of this verse. The suggestion that it is a letter Paul wrote from Laodicea seems most unlikely, as the insistence on the exchange of letters seems to presuppose that they were written about the same time. But Paul had been for some time in prison at Caesarea and Rome, so that the letter could not have been written at Laodicea. Was it then a letter written by the Laodicean Christians to Paul? This again seems unlikely. It is highly improbable that they would have kept a copy of a letter to him. Furthermore the very command to read this letter publicly strongly suggests that it is an apostolic message from Paul himself, rather than merely a letter from a church to him. Another suggestion which cannot be lightly ruled out is that there was a letter to Laodicea which has since been lost. But if there had been such a letter it would presumably have contained the usual greetings to the church. And if it was to be exchanged with the church at Colossae what would have been the point of including greetings to the Laodicean Christians in the Colossian letter?[2]

The most likely theory is that the letter in question was our canonical Epistle 'to the Ephesians'. It is usually accepted that this was not a letter to one church but was rather for wider circulation. Thus the title 'to the Ephesians' is absent from the best MSS and the words 'at Ephesus' of the first verse are likewise absent. The letter does not deal with a local situation but with truths which affect the Church at large. The bearer

---

[1] See Lightfoot's note, p. 272.
[2] See also the Introduction to Philemon.

of the letter is Tychicus (Eph. vi. 21) who also carried the letter to Colossae; and this together with the affinity between the two letters further confirms the view that they originated at the same time and went to the same area. If then the 'Ephesian' Epistle was sent to the churches in Asia Minor, it would most probably go to the large centre of Laodicea before being sent on to Colossae. It is quite possible that Paul uses the phrase *from Laodicea* simply because he puts himself in the position of those to whom he is writing, so that it is quite a natural designation for the letter.

17. For Lightfoot's suggestion that *Archippus* was ministering in Laodicea, see the comment on Philemon 2. It is difficult to be precise as to the particular form of *ministry* which had been committed to him. In view of the solemnity of the charge it was hardly the serving of tables. He may well have been in some position of pastoral oversight. Like every true minister of the gospel his commission is not from men but from the Lord. Indeed it was *in the Lord* that he received his ministry. It was because he was in living union with the Lord that his commission was directly given. But because of this very fact he must *take heed*. The word *blepe* speaks of being on the watch. It warns of dangers; and so we can see it against the background of the whole Epistle which warns of the perils of false teaching in the Church. He is to *fulfil* his ministry. The gift entrusted to him by the Lord is to be fully realized. The task of ministering in the church is to be discharged fully, without shirking any of the demands and without slacking.

18. The apostle gives his final farewell. His pen is in his own hands. It is a brief word, but in it there is an exquisite blend of the warm-hearted Paul and the authoritative apostle. In his *bonds* he desires their affectionate remembrance in prayer. But those same bonds are his because of the exercise of his apostolic ministry; and so the call to remember them is a call to submit to the authority of the one who writes, not as the prisoner of Caesar, but of Jesus Christ.

PHILEMON: ANALYSIS

I. INTRODUCTION (1–7).

    a. Salutation (1–3).

    b. Thanksgiving (4–7).

II. THE REQUEST (8–21).

    a. Paul's personal interest in Onesimus (8–14).

    b. Paul's plea for Onesimus (15–21).

III. CONCLUSION (22–25).

    a. Paul's proposed visit (22).

    b. Greetings (23–25).

PHILEMON: COMMENTARY

1. INTRODUCTION (1–7)

a. Salutation (1–3)

1. The gracious note which pervades this letter is struck at the outset in the greeting. Paul does not introduce himself as the apostle who has a right to demand obedience to his requests from a member of the Church. He is rather *a prisoner of Jesus Christ*, for it is the service of Christ which has led him into his present bondage. But it is this very fact which lends strength to the appeal he is about to make. He is not asking for a measure of sacrifice from Philemon, as one who knows nothing of sacrifice. He has forfeited his freedom for Christ's sake and so has a ground for appealing. This is a principle involved in any true pastoral work. The pastor can only appeal to his people for self-sacrifice and discipline if he himself knows the meaning of discipline in his own life. Otherwise his call is empty and lifeless.

2, 3. The close connection here between Archippus and Philemon and Apphia suggests that he was their son. Lightfoot's suggestion that Archippus was really ministering to the church at Laodicea seems quite likely. As he points out, the latter place was only a short distance from Colossae; and in the Epistle to Colossae the message to Archippus is included with the greetings sent via the Colossian Christians to the saints at Laodicea. One might object that if Archippus was really a pastor in Laodicea it would seem strange to send the greeting in such a roundabout way. But if we are right in assuming that the letter to Laodicea was the circular letter to the Ephesians, then there are no personal greetings in that letter and the message would, therefore, quite appropriately go via the neighbouring church at Colossae where Archippus' home was. Furthermore, the letter to Colossae was not related only to that centre; but might in a sense also be designated the letter to Laodicea, so that the message to Archippus in Colossians iv. 17 was really quite a direct one.

Again we see Paul's gracious attitude emerging as he puts the respective ministries of Philemon and Archippus alongside his own, describing them respectively as 'fellow-labourer' and *fellowsoldier*. It is not necessary to try and place these labours at one particular period of Paul's ministry, e.g. during his period at Ephesus. This does however seem likely to have been the time of Philemon's conversion; and judging by the obvious familiarity with both *Apphia and Archippus* it may well have been another case of household salvation. It is surely due to Paul's vivid awareness of the essential oneness of the Church of God. Distance and circumstances are secondary. They are united in a common service which means toil and conflict. For verse 3 see the note on Colossians i. 2.

b. Thanksgiving (4–7)

4. The apparently incidental inclusion of the personal *my* shows how much Paul's awareness of his covenant relationship with God has become part of his thinking. It is his confession of thanksgiving to the God of all grace who has stooped and entered into this relationship with one who is unworthy.

5. It is difficult to decide how to interpret this verse. It can be taken in three ways. It is possible to interpret *faith* as faithfulness; and the meaning would then be that Philemon's service for the Lord and His people is characterized by love and faithfulness. It is also possible to see here a chiasmus, i.e. a balanced grammatical structure in which the words at the extremes and those in the centre are grouped in pairs. This would link *love* with *toward all the saints* and *faith* with *toward the Lord Jesus*. There is however a third possibility, and that is to take both *love* and *faith* as being intimately knit in an attitude which is directed on the one hand to the Lord, and on the other to the saints. Love towards the Lord Jesus is linked closely with faith, for it is from faith that love grows, and by faith love is nourished. But the love which is shown towards the brethren is still love in the context of faith. It is not the ordinary love of the world. It is not evoked by something attractive in the other. It is a love which has its roots in faith in Christ; and the resultant attitude embraces the Lord and His people. The change of prepositions from 'toward' (*pros*) to 'unto' (*eis*) emphasizes that there is a difference in the two relationships. His love and faith are directed toward the Lord as its object; and it is this attitude to Him which reaches out through Him to fellow believers who are thus drawn as it were into a like relationship.

6. The interpretation suggested for verse 5 seems to be confirmed by the prayer here expressed. He desires that Philemon's *faith* in Christ, which we have seen to be linked with love, should be shared. His faith in Christ is to be no mere individual experience, but is to be a blessing to be enjoyed in common with others. Such a sharing should lead to a growth in knowledge, and indeed it is his prayer that it should be effective in promoting such. This knowledge, which Paul pictures as the outcome of faith, means a clear grasp of spiritual realities (see note on Col. i. 6). Here it is a grasp of all the blessings which are the Christian's heritage (lit. 'of all the good which is among us'). But at once he corrects any idea that such blessings are for the believer's personal enjoyment. He speaks rather in terms of blessings which have Christ as their goal (lit. 'unto Christ'). So he is praying for such a growth in knowledge of these blessings as will lead them to a deeper trust in Christ and obedience to Him. Here we see some characteristic elements in Paul's teaching. Faith is the source of knowledge. Faith grows into maturity in fellowship; and it is in that fellowship that there is a deepening in knowledge. (We may compare 1 Cor. iii. 1–3; Eph. i. 15–18, iii. 17–19, iv. 11–16; Col. ii. 2; 2 Thes. i. 3.) For a variety of interpretations of this verse see Lightfoot and C. F. D. Moule.

7. The *for* which introduces this verse points back to the expression of thanksgiving in verse 4 and gives a further reason for it. Here is a significant comment on Paul's keen awareness

of the unity of the body of Christ. He himself has not directly
benefited from Philemon's ministry. Yet he rejoices that other
believers have been blessed. We hear an echo of his word to
the Corinthians 'and whether one member suffer, all the
members suffer with it; or one member be honoured, all the
members rejoice with it' (1 Cor. xii. 26; cf. Rom. xii. 15).
We can see, too, Paul's humanity, for he not only rejoices but
he also finds *consolation*. The great apostle is not beyond the
need of strengthening. In his imprisonment, with all its
tendency to discouragement or depression, he has been
strengthened and encouraged by the grace of God manifested
in the life of Philemon.

II. THE REQUEST (8–21)

a. Paul's personal interest in Onesimus (8–14)

8, 9. His *wherefore* links the main matter of his letter with his
introductory remarks. These are not to be taken as just so
much preliminary small talk before he gets down to business,
for it is because of the love which has characterized Philemon's
life and witness, that Paul can write in the way he does. It is
because they move in an atmosphere of love that the request
can come, not in terms of an apostolic command to be
obeyed, but of a humble petition which calls for a willing
consent. Paul does not deny his apostolic authority. Indeed he
asserts that he has the courage to command Philemon; and
that courage is not because of some position of superiority
which he has wrongly arrogated to himself, for it is in *Christ*,
i.e. it springs from Paul's commission by the Lord. But *for
love's sake*, to avoid any possibility of marring the harmony, he
comes, not as the authoritative apostle, but as a suppliant (cf.
1 Cor. ix. 1–18). Here, incidentally, is an interesting comment
on Paul's frequent emphasis on his apostolic authority—an
emphasis which it is important to understand in any attempt to
formulate a doctrine of Scripture, as far as the New Testament
writings are concerned. The very fact that he is willing to for-
go his rightful claims as an apostle, shows that these claims
are not just due to a spiritual egotism. He does not insist on

standing on his dignity, for his personal position means nothing to him. This however makes his assertion of his apostolic authority all the stronger when he feels called on to insist on this in reply to those who would deny it in order to introduce false teaching (cf. Gal. i. 1, and see comment on Col. i. 1).

It is difficult to decide whether we should take it as *Paul the aged* or 'Paul, an ambassador' (RSV) (*presbutēs* or *presbeutēs*). The MS evidence favours the former; but Lightfoot points out that at this period *presbeutēs* was often written without the second 'e' so it would be quite valid to take it as 'ambassador'. In favour of this is the fact that Paul is writing to Philemon, who with a son in the ministry must have been somewhere near Paul's own age, and so a reference to age on Paul's part would hardly be as appropriate as it would were he writing to a younger man. Then too there is a close parallel in Ephesians vi. 20: 'an ambassador in bonds', and also in 2 Corinthians v. 20, where Paul speaks of the task of the ambassador as that of beseeching men, and uses the same word (*parakalō*) as here. To speak of himself as an ambassador would also continue the mode of presenting his case which he has adopted so far, namely the blend of authority with a gracious humility. He is an ambassador, but not one who arrogantly presents his claims, but rather brings his humble request. Then also, it would stand naturally with the further title *a prisoner of Jesus Christ* for, as we have seen, this is a title of honour and has also an implicit note of authority.

10. The affectionate reference to *Onesimus* is typical of the warm bond of love which existed between Paul and his converts. It is a comment too on what the grace of God had wrought in the apostle himself. This is the one-time self-righteous Pharisee, the heir of Jewish exclusiveness, and he is speaking of a Gentile, and a Gentile slave at that, from the very dregs of Roman society—yet he can refer to him as a *son*. So his statement (Col. iii. 11) that 'there is neither Greek nor Jew . . . bond nor free' is no empty formula but reflects the attitude of heart to which he himself has been brought by God.

11. There is a pun here on the name Onesimus which means 'useful'. So Paul adds that formerly he was useless, but is now for the first time useful. His new-found usefulness is due to his new-found faith. The *but now* marks the radical difference between what he was before and what he is now since his conversion. He is *profitable* to Philemon, for instead of the slave who formerly gave the grudging service of those who obeyed 'with eyeservice, as menpleasers', now he has learnt as a Christian to serve 'in singleness of heart, fearing God' (Col. iii. 22, 23). But we must not limit Onesimus' usefulness to his new attitude to his work. Paul adds that not only is he profitable to Philemon, but also to himself. Presumably he means that the devotion which his spiritual child showed him was a comfort to him; and this was a token of what he would be to Philemon—to Paul a son, and to Philemon a beloved brother in Christ.

12–14. Paul introduces a further note here as he speaks of what it cost him to send Onesimus back; and how he would gladly have retained him. In sending him he has sent part of himself. But he gently points out at the same time that in a sense he would have been justified in keeping Onesimus with him to minister in Philemon's stead. Here is the hint which will later be openly stated, that Philemon is in debt to the apostle because of what he has received from him in terms of spiritual blessing. So Paul has a right to expect a return in terms of service; and this could have been rendered by Onesimus on Philemon's behalf. But he did not retain Onesimus for he does not want Philemon to offer such service from a sense of duty, but from a willing heart. This recalls Paul's teaching about Christian giving. The Christian has a duty to give; and yet the Lord does not want him to give 'grudgingly, or of necessity: for God loveth a cheerful giver' (2 Cor. ix. 7).

b. Paul's plea for Onesimus (15–21)

15. Now the argument moves on to another plane, as Paul introduces the thought of God's providential ordering of circumstances. He puts it in a tentative fashion; but this is surely only because of the tactful approach he is making. We cannot imagine any doubt as to God's sovereign overruling in one who could say, 'We know that all things work together for good to them that love God' (Rom. viii. 28). But instead of a dogmatic assertion, he puts the same truth in the form of a gracious suggestion. It recalls Mordecai's words to Esther 'who knoweth whether thou art come to the kingdom for such a time as this?' (Est. iv. 14). So while he was fully aware that Onesimus' departure from Philemon had been deliberate, he sees the hand of God in it, and speaks of him as having been parted. The AV misses this point by translating it as an active (*he departed*) though the verb is in the passive. Onesimus with all his wilfulness had been, unknown to himself, in the hand of the sovereign God. To appreciate fully the reality of divine providence, it is essential to look at events from the eternal standpoint. To dwell only on the present situation is to fail to see how what is apparently adverse is being moulded by God to His purposes. So Paul contrasts the brief period of Onesimus' departure, which must in many ways have seemed a most unfortunate occurrence, with the eventual outcome, which was a reunion that would never be ended, not even by death.

16. Paul has spoken in the previous verse of Philemon's receiving restitution—the word used for 'receive' (*apechō*) suggests the payment of a sum of money. Now he shows what is involved in this restitution. Philemon had lost a slave and has received in return more than a slave, namely *a brother* in Christ. Note that Paul does not deny that Onesimus is still a slave. He does not say, 'not now a servant', but *not now as a servant*. He still is a slave; but he is no longer to be treated as one, for the old relationship of master and slave is absorbed into the new one of brethren. The brother stands on a higher level for he is *above a servant*. Indeed Paul takes it even further. Philemon is not just to accord him a privileged position as a fellow Christian. He is to love him; and the intensity of that love is shown by the way Paul, as it were, moves one degree higher than a superlative. He says that Onesimus is beloved most of all to him; and then adds that he is even more than 'most of all' to Philemon. Paul has him at the level of Christian fellowship, while Philemon has him both on the human level (*in the flesh*) as a transformed servant, and on the spiritual level (*in the Lord*) as a *brother beloved*.

17-19. Paul now puts his request quite firmly; and yet he still blends the firmness with the personal note. If he really is Philemon's *partner*, that is to say, if they really share together in the blessings and work of the gospel, then doubtless Philemon would be glad to welcome his fellow-worker. Let him then welcome Onesimus in just the same way, for in so doing he will be receiving the apostle himself.

In asking for mercy for Onesimus, Paul does not ignore the past. Philemon had been injured, probably because of theft by the runaway slave. Restitution must be made; and Paul himself pledges himself as the guarantor for the repayment of the debt. But having done so, he then sets alongside the debt he now owes to Philemon, the far greater debt Philemon owes to him; for in owing to Paul his conversion, he owes to him his very life. Clearly Paul implies, although in a rather gentle way, that Onesimus' debt which he has taken over is more than cancelled.

20. The final request is again lifted to a new level by the phrase *in the Lord*. He wants a benefit from Philemon, that is he wants him to give him cause for rejoicing. But that *joy* would be *in the Lord* for it would spring from the realization that it was the Lord who had enabled His servant to act in a magnanimous way. So too the refreshment of heart which Paul desires is *in the Lord* (RV 'in Christ'). He will not merely be encouraged on the human level. Because the response to his request will be a spiritual one due to the blessings of the gospel which Philemon has experienced, in short, because the expected generosity is due to Philemon's new life in Christ, Paul will be really encouraged, for it will be a fresh reminder of what it means to be in Christ. From seeing the life of Christ manifest in the action of Philemon, he himself will be led back to the same rich resources of power.

21. He reinforces his request in two ways. In the first place he assumes Philemon will act as he has asked. It is a wise approach to a fellow Christian to expect the highest from him rather than to be content with the second-rate. In the second place, he mentions the visit he hopes to pay shortly and obviously this is an added incentive.

He says he is confident Philemon will *do more* than he has asked. But what more could he do? The only answer would seem to be the granting of complete freedom. But it is significant that the nearest approach to a request for manumission comes only as a hint. At this point, if Paul were going to insist on slavery being wrong, and on Philemon's duty to free Onesimus, he would surely have done so. But he does not attack the institution. Instead, if Philemon carries out not only in letter but in spirit the terms of the apostle's request, the status of Onesimus will matter little, for he will move into the liberty of Christian fellowship. (See Introduction, p. 24.)

III. CONCLUSION (22-25)

a. Paul's proposed visit (22)

22. The duty of hospitality was strongly enjoined on believers as we may see from various references in the Epistles (Rom. xii. 13; 1 Tim. iii. 2; Tit. i. 8; Heb. xiii. 2; 1 Pet. iv. 9). This is reflected in the very natural way in which Paul here asks for accommodation to be provided for him.

b. Greetings (23-25)

23-25. The apostle has asked much. He will end with a greeting which is also a prayer. The Lord Jesus Christ who gave infinitely much to redeem Philemon will give him grace to perform all that has been asked and more. But in this final greeting Paul reverts to the plural—*your* spirit (*humōn*). This is a letter not only to Philemon but to the church. The grace of the Lord Jesus will be theirs also to teach the same lesson of love, and to produce the same spirit of obedience.